Pig Keeping

Richard Lutwyche

Pig Keeping

*Inspiration and practical advice
for would-be smallholders*

 National Trust

First published in the United Kingdom in 2010 by
National Trust Books
10 Southcombe Street
London W14 0RA
An imprint of Anova Books Company Ltd

ISBN 9781905400867

A CIP catalogue for this book is available from the British Library.

15 14 13 12 11 10
10 9 8 7 6 5 4 3 2 1

Reproduction by Mission Productions Ltd, Hong Kong.
Printed and bound by WS Bookwell OY, Finland

This book can be ordered direct from the publisher at the website
www.anovabooks.com, or try your local bookshop. Also available
at National Trust shops, including www.nationaltrustbooks.co.uk.

The information contained in this book is not a substitute for specialist
advice on specific issues concerning pig keeping. Neither the publishers,
the National Trust nor the author make any warranties or representations
regarding the accuracy of material contained herein and exclude liability
to the fullest extent permitted by law for any consequence resulting
from reliance upon it. Reasonable care has been taken to ensure that
information relating to laws and regulations reflects the general state of
the law as understood by the author at the time of going to press. Any
liability for inaccuracies or errors contained herein is expressly excluded
to the fullest extent permitted by law. If you intend to rear and keep pigs
for any purpose you must contact DERFA as well as your local Animal
Welfare Office and ensure that you comply with all applicable legislation.

CONTENTS

PREFACE

My aim in writing this little book is to try to impart information to the novice pig keeper – the hobby farmer or smallholder. It pulls no punches. This is not an idyllic description of porcine heaven but a reality check of all that's involved in keeping pigs.

If you get to the end and feel I'm being too negative, well, so be it. The intention is to make you think before you commit. Don't get me wrong: pigs are wonderful animals, but it's because I think so highly of them that I do not want anyone planning to keep them without careful consideration. Not only do you have intelligent creatures to care for; if you follow my advice and keep some of the rare breeds, then you have a living part of our heritage to look after too.

If you do start keeping pigs on a small scale, then be prepared for them to take over a large part of your life. They will become the first things you think about in the morning and the last things you think about at night. Their wellbeing, comfort and welfare should be put before your own. If you can't get cover in order to go on holiday, then cancel your holiday. If a gilt's farrowing clashes with your team's football match on the telly, set the video recorder – your pigs can't wait. If a pal says let's go shopping or let's go to the pub, make sure your chores are done first. The pigs must be fed and tended to before your pleasure can be considered.

That's why I start off by asking you to question your commitment. Throughout the book you need to note the level of work and amount of time that you must dedicate to looking after your pigs. Do that and they should reward you handsomely – not financially, but in terms of companionship and satisfaction at a job well done. You will come to understand what a wonderful dish real pork is and to appreciate quality food from animals that have enjoyed the best existence possible.

I have tried to include all the legal issues you should be aware of but bear in mind that there can be a lot of red tape involved in keeping pigs. Things may well have changed by the time you read this, so make sure you study the relevant websites and publications to keep up to date with legislation.

COMMITMENT

It may seem strange opening the first chapter by asking whether you have thought through the idea of keeping pigs. But believe me, I find it distressing when someone contacts me, having been so full of enthusiasm, asking for help to get rid of their pigs because they had not realised how much commitment was involved. So, please do think carefully about the following.

Pigs appeal to many people, usually when they see a small piglet; but little pigs grow – very rapidly – and have some very demanding needs. Unlike sheep, beef cattle and horses, pigs do not graze grass and cannot be left in a field to fend for themselves; they need a balanced diet that the pig keeper must supply – preferably twice a day. Even if you feed them only once a day, pigs need to be inspected at least twice daily. They also need ready access to clean, fresh water at all times. That's usually quite easy for most of the year but how you will cope when there's a foot of snow on the ground and the hosepipe is frozen solid?

Outdoor pigs need strong, secure fencing. They are large animals that root the ground and will quickly discover any weakness in the perimeter. They have a lively enquiring mind and love nothing better than to explore in search of something good to eat.

Consider how you will cope during holidays or when you are unwell. Finding someone to look after your pig(s) is not easy, so you need to take that into account.

Pigs are farm animals and come with a heap of red tape that you must take on board, even if you only intend to keep one, or preferably two, as pets. Because they can spread serious diseases, such as Foot and Mouth or swine fever, the government keeps a very close watch on them and your premises will have to be registered as a livestock holding before you bring a pig onto the property. To do this you need a County Parish Holding (CPH) number from the Rural Payments Agency (see Useful Addresses, page 90). In addition, you need to make a separate registration of the fact that you have livestock and be issued with a herd mark, however small your 'herd'! You will be able to do this with your local Animal Health Office – contact details are listed in *A Guide for New Keepers: Pigs* (see Further Reading, page 93)

Whenever another pig (or other farm animal) moves onto the property, your stock will be subject to a six or 20 day standstill, depending on the species. Pigs arriving on your holding mean that other pigs may not leave your holding for 20 days. Cattle, sheep and goats may not leave your holding for 6 days. This applies to shows, markets, movements for breeding and so on. The only exception is for any stock moving directly to an abattoir or an approved isolation unit. Even when the ban on moving your pigs is lifted, you have to fill out a Movement Licence, which has to be sent to the Local Authority for your area. To keep proper records you will need a Movement Book and a supply of AML2 Movement Licences, which can be obtained from your local Trading Standards Office.

You'll also need to keep a Medicines Register showing all medicines administered and the withdrawal dates – when an animal has been given medicine, a certain period of time must elapse before the animal can be slaughtered and go into the food chain. Officials can demand to inspect both the Movement Records and Medicines Register at almost any time.

It's not yet mandatory to keep a Feed Register but stock keepers are increasingly being asked for one, so it would be better to be prepared. It should show the volume and sort of feed given to each type of pig, including any 'extras' such as fruit and vegetables. As part of this record, file the tags from the feed bags and so on, showing the composition of all bought-in feed.

Finally, again because of the disease risk, pigs are subject to strict controls during any outbreak of what is called a 'notifiable disease' such as classical or African swine fever, Foot and Mouth disease, Aujeszky's disease or swine vesicular disease – for a full list see *A Guide for New Keepers: Pigs* (see Further Reading, page 93). Even if your pigs are unaffected, the government reserves the right to come onto your property and slaughter all of them if they believe it may help to restrict the spread of the disease. Not a pretty thought, but the authorities have to look at the bigger picture.

So, having tried to make you aware of the situation in a realistic way, I hope you are prepared to share your life with what are generally very endearing and intelligent animals. Pig keeping can easily become addictive.

PET PIGS

Now, I'm going to start off being negative again because pigs aren't really suitable as pets in the same way as dogs, cats or goldfish are. That doesn't mean to say that you cannot keep pigs in a good-sized garden. But if you're thinking about having a pig to take on a lead to the shops or the local pub or have sitting in the back of your car – DON'T!

Pigs are farmyard animals developed for meat production. They are herd animals and are not necessarily happy being kept on their own. Yes, there are instances of people keeping pigs as pets but many end in disaster and that's what I want to avoid by writing this book.

If you do want a pig as a pet, many of the official hoops still have to be jumped through. You still need a County Parish Holding (CPH) number and a herd mark (see page 9 for more information), however small your 'herd'!

WALKING THE PIG

If you are keeping a pig as a pet, you can apply to your local Animal Health Office for a special licence to allow you to walk your pig(s) along a specified route. That route cannot be close to other pig farms, livestock markets or food outlets. Once you've got a licence, you cannot deviate from the route, however keen your pet might be to explore a new by-way. The licence needs to be renewed annually. In the event of an outbreak of Foot and Mouth or some other contagious disease, the right to walk your pig may be withdrawn without notice.

All pigs are subject to laws about what can be fed to them. Many people have romantic ideas about feeding a pig on kitchen scraps (or swill) as an ultimate method of recycling, but giving them any food waste from a kitchen (domestic, industrial or even vegetarian), is strictly forbidden. This is because there is a strong risk of spreading diseases such as Foot and Mouth and Swine Fever through food that has been in close proximity to meat or meat products derived from infected animals. Such diseases exist in Eastern Europe, Asia, Africa and South America and, while we humans cannot be infected by eating contaminated meat, animals such as pigs can. I'm old enough to remember when swill feeding was widespread – during World War II, when the practice was at its zenith, swill was known as Tottenham Pudding – and the bad press that pigs got as smelly creatures was largely due to the feed in those days, which affected not only the pigs but their keepers too.

KEEP THE HOUSE OUT OF BOUNDS

Pet pigs should not be allowed into the house. A pig will wallow in mud in even just barely warm weather – not because it is a filthy creature but as a means of protection from over-heating and sunburn. Like dogs, pigs don't sweat; they control their temperature through panting and a wet nose but, being much larger than dogs, they need to take additional measures and a wallow is a good way of cooling down.

Pigs are intelligent and can easily get bored. This can result in pet pigs who are kept indoors destroying carpets and furniture. One Vietnamese Pot Belly kept in a London flat destroyed and largely consumed its owners' sofa. Others have flooded houses by chewing through water pipes.

So, please don't keep a pig as a cute and cuddly pet. It doesn't fit the bill. By all means keep pigs for fattening or breeding, which I shall cover in later chapters. Either way, you will be thoroughly rewarded in terms of the pleasure derived. As for the financial rewards, there are very few pig keepers in Britain making money out of them. If you're thinking of keeping pigs as a route to an exotic retirement on a sunny Caribbean island in a few years' time, I think you may be disappointed.

PIGS FOR MEAT

Enthusiasts on television and in the media, such as Hugh Fearnley-Whittingstall, have done much to inspire people who would like to keep some form of livestock on a small scale. There are many different reasons for wishing to do so.

One of the most common is having 'control' over how your meat is produced and enjoying the reassurance of knowing that your stock have enjoyed a contented and fulfilled life, leading to delicious, healthy meat. The alternative of buying mass-produced meat from the supermarkets depresses many people – and rightly so.

Others can include the more practical, such as using pigs to turn over and clear scrubland – with the 'harvest' at the end of their lives an added bonus.

You might keep pigs to help educate your children to the realities of life, as most children have little concept of how their sausages and bacon are produced. Certainly, it was not many generations ago that nearly all country people had a pig in a sty to keep them supplied with meat during the winter. In the first half of the 19th century, William Cobbett, in his book *Rural Rides*, recorded life in Stroud in Gloucestershire:

> *'The people seem to be constantly well off. A pig in almost every cottage sty; and that is the infallible mark of a happy people.'*

In our regulated, industrialised lives we seem to yearn to get back to nature and a simpler way of life.

Whatever your reason, you must consider the practicalities and comments discussed in the previous chapters. Also, make sure there are no by-laws or restrictions in tenancy agreements against keeping livestock on your premises. Take into account, too, what impact it may have on your neighbours and how they will react. A friendly wave and 'hullo' today may soon turn sour if your next-door neighbours object to the sounds, smell or sight of your pigs. Be aware of religious sensitivities: Jews and Muslims believe pigs are unclean and may be offended by what you consider to be an animal of great charm. Although you may pooh-pooh the idea, nothing raises objections more than the idea that someone's property might be devalued because of your hobby: so think carefully before you commit, and talk to your neighbours about your plans. Providing they do not have religious objections, nor are vegans or vegetarians, a pound of home-produced sausages or a couple of pork chops every now and then may help to overcome opposition. Remember that PR is a powerful tool: at all stages of pig keeping, keep those who might object onside if at all possible. You may think they are being awkward but if they complain to the authorities, they can make your life very difficult indeed.

ACCOMMODATION

Now we come on to what you need to do, having decided to go ahead and keep a pig or two for meat. Firstly, let's look at space issues.

Pigs in commercial indoor units can end up with very little space, but you are trying to get away from industrial farming so giving the pigs enough room is important. Two small weaners at eight weeks old won't require very much room but four months later when they reach pork weight – around 70–75kg (150–165lb) each – their needs will be different.

Are the pigs going to be kept inside or out? If you have a semi-open barn, this could be ideal and will save you adding extra fencing or worrying about the effects on your ground of having lively animals that root rather than graze. Make sure there are no gaps that could become escape routes and put plenty of clean straw down in a suitable bedding area. If the barn is very open, try to find a sheltered spot out of draughts and driving rain for the sleeping quarters or even consider making a simple shelter within the building.

A traditional pig sty (a closed building for sleeping with an enclosure on the front for eating, dunging and exercise) can be suitable but may not provide enough space for exercise. If not, perhaps the pigs could be let out for an hour a day to scamper and play, returning to the enclosure just in time for feeding (pigs will need a reason to curtail their freedom). Alternatively, give them some toys to exercise with, such as a very robust football or a small tyre suspended on a rope, making sure that it is set in such a way that none of the pigs can get caught in the centre of the tyre.

How much space will they need if kept outside? There's no simple answer. Your soil type and the time of year will affect your decision. The Department for Environment, Food and Rural Affairs (DEFRA) advises a maximum stocking rate of 25 sows to the hectare but that's pretty academic when you're planning a pen for a couple of weaners. Pigs kept on a light, sandy soil can usually stay in the same area for months without a problem. The same pigs on heavy clay in winter will turn a small area into a quagmire in very little time. While I approve of keeping pigs outside, I am sure that they do not enjoy wading about up to their bellies in thick, heavy mud in cold conditions. If you have the space, divide the area you have set aside for pigs into two or three runs so that they can be moved to fresh ground as needed before the conditions become intolerable.

Outdoor pigs can successfully be kept in woodlands but be aware that once the scrubby vegetation has been cleared, the pigs may well turn to damaging trees by removing bark and should be moved to another area before this happens.

Ground heavily infested with bracken can be dangerous to pigs. Bracken is carcinogenic and over time pigs can develop tumours from eating the fern-like plant and die. Although some people swear by pigs as a means of clearing bracken, do be warned that repeated exposure can be disastrous.

FENCING FOR OUTDOOR PIGS

The next aspect to consider once you have determined your site, is fencing. Your fencing must be robust if it is not to be breached. Pigs are superstar escape artists – they will find the merest chink in their boundaries and go off exploring. Don't think for a moment that stuffing a few branches into the weaker parts of a hedge will ever be a way of keeping pigs confined. Invest time and money in quality fencing and do the job properly.

I would recommend strong pig netting buried 15cm (6in) into the ground with a single strand of barbed wire set about 10–15cm (4–6in) above the ground level. You can certainly use electric fencing and I would suggest a double-wire system set around 15cm and 30cm (6in and 12in) above ground. However, some pigs, once they have experienced the (mild) shock, usually through their snout, may be so traumatised that they refuse to cross the boundary to leave the enclosure when you need them too. Others seem to be oblivious to electric fences and, certainly with some adults, the sight of a potential mate seems to outweigh the effects of the shock. Electric fences need more attention than other systems: there are batteries to recharge if the system is not mains operated; and grass and weeds need to be trimmed regularly or they will short-out the fence where they touch it.

Although it may seem unnecessary for just a couple of pigs kept for pork production, I would always build a small corral inside the gate to make loading easier (see colour section for illustration). That way, when the time comes to load up the pigs for the journey to the abattoir, you can lure them into the corral by feeding them there. It is also useful if a pig needs veterinary attention or as a failsafe for getting in and out through the gate without letting boisterous pigs escape.

However much pigs enjoy the outdoor life, it is important
that they have a dry, weatherproof shelter to retreat to in bad
weather and for sleeping in. The simplest solution is to buy
a pig ark. This is a small, often moveable (on rails) shelter
made of wood, wood and corrugated iron or, nowadays,
plastic. It can be either straight-sided in a triangular form
(seen from the front) or have a semi-circular shape (see
below and colour section for illustration). If possible, get
one with a wooden floor for maximum comfort for the pigs.
There are disadvantages to those made of corrugated iron,
which can heat up like ovens on a hot summer's day and will
retain some of that heat when the pigs turn in at night. Site
the ark facing away from the prevailing wind, on an area
unlikely to flood or to be in the path of any impromptu
stream forming in heavy rain.

Arks can be bought new or secondhand. The internet will
find you a whole variety at various prices, both new and
old, and don't ignore the auction sites. If you are looking for
secondhand ones, check the farming papers and ask local
auctioneers whether any are being offered in farm sales.

You can, of course, build your own ark or shelter. You can make a very serviceable building for pigs using small straw bales for the walls, reinforced inside and out with pig netting, and held up by a few stout fence posts. Use corrugated iron or a strong marine plywood for the roof. This has the advantage that by removing the roof and the wire netting, the remainder is fully biodegradable when its useful life has come to an end. I have known such shelters to last a number of years.

On both types of shelter, I would recommend hanging an old hessian sack over the doorway to make the interior as snug as possible for the inhabitants. If you are building an ark or other house, don't make it too compact or low. Remember that a pig may fall ill and you, and perhaps a vet, will have to go inside to treat it. It's not much fun doing that on your hands and knees because the roof's too low!

To keep the housing clean and tidy you will need a wheelbarrow, muck fork, stiff-bristled yard broom, shovel and disinfectant in bulk, plus a supply of clean straw and somewhere dry to store it (see colour section for illustration).

WATER SUPPLY

Next to consider is a water supply. If you keep the pigs close to the house, you may decide that a hosepipe or even a bucket will suffice but pigs have a huge thirst for drinking water and you must ensure that they always have enough clean water. They need checking regularly too: a water trough can become a good game and the contents could be tipped out 10 minutes after you've filled it up. You can't leave even small pigs without water for many hours, especially in warmer weather.

Talking of hot weather, outdoor pigs must either have plenty of shelter (such as dense woodland), or you must provide a wallow for them, which will need water adding on a daily basis. All this means is a muddy area they can excavate and make a nice pool to bury themselves in. This is a method of cooling the body but also helps to prevent sunburn. It also helps remove parasites such as lice.

If the pigs are some distance away from an existing water supply, you must plan how to make your life easier. If it is a chore to water the pigs, then sooner or later it won't get done and the pigs will suffer. You can get a water bowser on wheels, which can be parked next to the pen or field as your source. Modern equivalents are plastic tanks in wire cages, which can be mounted on a trailer to similar effect. Probably the best solution, though, is to lay an alkathene pipe from a mains supply as a semi-permanent solution. This is stronger than a hosepipe and less susceptible to damage. It is also more (but not totally) resistant to freezing – a major problem for the pig keeper in the depths of winter.

CHOOSING LIVESTOCK

You've got your CPH number, you've registered that you're keeping livestock (see page 9), you've prepared the building or enclosure where the pigs will live and sorted out your water supply. It's time to get some pigs!

NOW GET YOUR PIGS

Whether you're just planning to fill your freezer or start an enterprise selling home-produced pork or bacon, the selection of your pigs is of paramount importance. The pigs used to supply the supermarkets are industrially grown super-hybrids, carefully selected by teams of white-coated scientists for rapid growth and an ultra-lean carcase. Unfortunately, the resulting meat is all but tasteless.

For the type of small-scale production we are talking about here, I strongly suggest that you source young pigs from one of the rare breeds, all of which are described on pages 58–65. Our rare breeds became rare in the post-war years because they wouldn't adapt to intensive farming methods. Successful breeds such as the Large White and Landrace were better suited and filled the market needs, while most of the remaining breeds languished. Some, such as the Cumberland, the Dorset Gold Tip and the Lincolnshire Curly Coat became extinct, gone forever. Others came perilously close to extinction but have been saved, so that you can begin keeping them and enjoy the real taste of delicious pork as it should be.

Our rare breeds still need all the help they can get. If you go out and buy a few weaners to fatten, you will encourage more people to keep more of them and their numbers will go up.

Finding local breeders should not be a major problem unless you are living in a very remote spot; nearly all the breeders' clubs have websites listing members by region. The British Pig Association (BPA), which is the registration authority for most breeds, has a website with details of who has young stock available by region. Alternatively, you can check advertisements in smallholding and farming magazines. See Useful Addresses (page 90) for more information.

You might have a particular favourite in mind when selecting a breed, something that appeals to you – whether it's the colour, the cute snout on a Middle White or a breed's reputation for delicious meat. Whatever the reason, stick to your original choice, at least with your first pigs. You can always try a different breed next time.

Once you've made contact with someone who has suitable pigs for sale, go and have a look at them; interrogate the breeder about his or her pigs, their husbandry methods and garner as much information as possible. There's always something new to learn and talking to experienced pig people can be rewarding.

Go to see the pigs with a strict number in mind. With all the planning you've done, don't be persuaded into taking more pigs than you want to. If your first pigs become a chore, you'll lose your enthusiasm and the chances are all your hard work will go to waste.

You should be selecting weaners at around 8–12 weeks old. Providing you are only planning on fattening the pigs – and not showing or breeding from them – it does not matter that they don't meet the breed standard in terms of markings, ear set, head shape or the number of teats. What you must look for is well-grown, sturdy, strong pigs with a bright eye and a bold disposition. Don't be tempted by the cute little runt that hides behind his siblings. He or she will rarely grow well and will end up costing more in feed and management, so don't be guided by your heart. Avoid any pigs that are coughing or with runny eyes or noses or signs of scouring (diarrhoea). Check for hernias – umbilical or genital hernias can be detected by a visible soft swelling – and reject any pigs that you find with them.

MALE OR FEMALE?

One thing to consider is the sex of the pigs. Females (gilts) will be fine but the breeder will almost always have more boars than gilts for sale because good gilts can be kept or sold for breeding, which makes them more valuable. Very few people castrate boars nowadays so you need to be aware of what having 'entire' boars entails. For pork, you will be keeping the pigs until they are 26–28 weeks old and for bacon another 6–10 weeks on top of that. If you are keeping boars and gilts together, even litter siblings, you will find that the boars start becoming sexually precocious after about 16–18 weeks of age, sometimes younger. This means that they will try to 'ride' the females (and sometimes the males); for this reason many people prefer to keep their fattening pigs in single-sex units. When they start this behaviour they are not sexually mature but they can become fertile at around six months old, making it even more of a problem.

Another consideration is what is known as 'boar taint'. This is totally random and quite rare but, once experienced, never forgotten. Many breeders and keepers of pigs will tell you that it's an old wives' tale and has never happened to them but, believe me, it isn't. I have known a top London restaurant, owned by a celebrity chef, with an open-plan kitchen viewed by the diners, literally empty one Sunday lunchtime when the stink from an infected joint killed all the anticipation of fine dining. The owner was not amused! For more information on boar taint see Further Reading (page 93).

24

Even though it is a slight risk, which is often only detected when a piece of meat from such a carcase is cooking, I would strongly suggest that if you are taking pigs to heavier weights than pork (around 70kg), you only buy gilts or castrated boars. If you keep boars on to higher weights for bacon (90–120kg), this will coincide with sexual maturity and there is a greater chance of taint as a consequence. For ease of management, if you can, buy groups of single-sex pigs for pork production.

TRANSPORTING PIGS

Before you can take your pigs home, the vendor will need to complete and give you an Animal Movement Licence and include your CPH number, so take note of it and bring it with you. You too will have to complete your own movement licences each and every time a pig or other farm animal moves off your premises, however briefly. To find out more about these, contact your local Trading Standards Officer.

Invariably, there are restrictions on the transport of live pigs; you can't just shoo them into the back of your car. You should have a ventilated livestock trailer with a loading ramp and side gates, which should be pristinely clean and disinfected since it was last used. If your destination is more than 65km (just over 40 miles) away, you need a special licence to transport livestock for 'economic activity'. The licence is obtained by sitting a written exam, but you should check whether this is required for your own use. It might be easier to pay extra and have the breeder deliver the pigs to you. If you do use your own trailer, make sure your motor insurance covers such use.

FEEDING PIGS

One way or another, you've got your pigs home and into
their run. One of the pieces of information you need from the
breeder is their current feed regime. You may be lucky and be
given their first feed as part of the deal. But now it's down to
you to source the appropriate pig food. By sticking to what
the breeder fed, there's no chance of upsetting your pigs'
appetite or digestive system.

THE RIGHT FEED

Unless you are already farming your own wheat and barley,
I'm assuming that you're going to be buying your pig feed
ready mixed. For just a few pigs, it is not usually worth bulk
buying from the feed mills, which would involve investing in
a storage silo into which a tonne or more of loose feed is
delivered at a time. Instead you should be thinking about
buying feed from a farm merchant in 20kg or 25kg (45lb
or 55lb) bags.

Hybrid pigs used in commercial farming eat a high-powered
Grower Ration with a protein level of 20% or more, but this
will be wasted on the slower-growing rare breeds. I suggest
you choose a more suitable Sow and Weaner mix with a lower
protein content of 16–18%.

The feed can come as a dry powder or meal, which can be fed
dry but is better mixed with water to make a more appetising
paste. The wet feed needs to be fed from a trough or other
container. The dry meal is better fed this way too – if scattered
on the ground, it can blow around in windy weather.

More commonly the feed is sold as pellets, which can be scattered on the ground – preferably not into thick mud or puddles – or placed in a trough. Sometimes feed can be obtained as larger cobs, which are equally suitable for scattering but are most appropriate for adult pigs.

You'll need vermin-proof storage for loose feed: the blue coloured plastic containers with black screw lids for fruit juices are very handy – they are often sold at shows.

You may feel that you can feed your pigs on the cheap without buying ready-made pig feed derived from cereals with added protein (usually soya beans). Indeed, historically pigs rarely enjoyed such luxury but our knowledge of their needs has changed: pigs have a digestive system very close to our own and need a balanced diet of carbohydrates, protein, vitamins and minerals. I am assuming you want a quality end-product in terms of yield and taste, and a balanced diet is the most likely way of achieving that. Treating pigs as scavengers and feeding them mostly or entirely on whey, waste vegetables or bread waste is likely to lead to variation in growth, poorer muscle development and excess fat.

That does not mean that you cannot supplement their diet with some tasty morsels like sugar or fodder beet, vegetables and fruit from the garden, but make sure that the basics are in place first. However, before you start feeding extras, please read and abide by the information given in the chapter on Pet Pigs (see page 11). You cannot feed them anything that's come out of a kitchen of any sort and certainly nothing that's been in contact with meat or meat products. If you're offered bakery waste as a supplement, make sure it doesn't include anything that may have been contaminated with pizzas, sausage rolls or even lardy cake! If in doubt, don't use it.

Although pigs have a reputation for being greedy, they can be quite fussy eaters and in my time I have known pigs to reject onions, oranges, lemons and grapefruits, peppers and even raw potatoes.

HOW MUCH?

The next question is how much to feed the pigs. From weaners to animals up to 40kg (88lb) in weight, it's best to feed *ad lib* if you can. That means having a self-service hopper where the individual pigs lift a flap to access their meal or pellets as often and whenever they like. For animals up to 40kg (88lb), this should be fine and, despite their reputation, they are unlikely to over-eat. The additional benefit of a self-service hopper is that weaker, smaller pigs can eat in peace without having to compete at an open trough with larger, stronger siblings.

From 40kg (88lb) up, you will need to restrict the pigs' intake to ensure they don't get too fat – about 1.8kg (4lb) a day per pig. The best way of deciding the amount is to monitor what they will eat at a 20-minute 'sitting'. If they've licked their troughs clean in under 20 minutes, they need a little more; if there's uneaten food after 20 minutes, then they're getting too much. As the pigs get closer to their ultimate weight of 70–75kg (150–165lb), up the daily rate to 2kg (5lb).

I have been talking glibly about weights, but if you're only going into pigs in a small way then there's no justification for getting an expensive set of pig-weighing scales. So how can you get an idea of a pig's actual weight? Measure the girth of the pig's chest just behind the shoulders in inches. Then measure the length of the pig from the base of the ears to the root of the tail, again in inches. Multiply the two measurements together and divide the result by 13, 12 or 11 depending on whether the pig is lean, medium or fat respectively. The resulting figure is roughly the weight in pounds (divide by 2.2 to convert to kilograms).

THE FINAL CURTAIN

You need to take this aspect into account. Where is the nearest suitable abattoir? You can get a list of licensed slaughterhouses from the Food Standards Agency, which will show the location and which species they slaughter. But just because there is a pig abattoir within a reasonable distance, doesn't necessarily solve your problems – you need to do more research.

The large industrial units that supply the supermarkets, for instance, cannot cope with someone turning up in a car and trailer with just two (or even 10) pigs. They are geared up to deal with fleets of 40-tonne lorries with pigs crammed in on three levels and, frankly, your treasured porkers would get lost in the system. So you need to find a small- or medium-sized abattoir that will deal with what are known as 'private kills'.

And not all abattoirs are the same. There are good and not quite so good. Yes, they are highly regulated and inspected beyond all reasonable levels, but are they helpful and friendly to deal with? Do they handle the pigs in a sympathetic way *en route* to the slaughter hall? To the best of my knowledge,

Which? magazine has never done a survey on abattoirs so it's a case of local knowledge. Ask farmers in the area and maybe ask for help on some of the forums on farming and smallholding websites.

Of course, there are so few abattoirs around nowadays that you may not have the luxury of picking and choosing. Most parts of England are still reasonably well served but there are gaps. Welsh and Scottish smallholders can face huge journeys to the nearest facility, making a nonsense of any financial planning.

Before you deliver pigs to the abattoir for the first time, you will need to complete and submit a Food Chain Information (FCI) form, which the abattoir should supply you with. Thereafter, on each subsequent visit, a simpler form must be completed.

ONE LAST WARNING

I've kept this to the end because it's something you must consider very carefully. You may think you already have but believe me I come across this *so often* that it makes your mind boggle. Think about it very carefully.

In the section on selecting your pig, I advised that you don't need to take account of pedigree issues such as correct markings, good underlines (teats), and so on. You certainly should not be choosing quality pedigree pigs just to fatten for pork or bacon. However, I come across the following scenario so often that I urge you to think very carefully before you commit to buying your first pigs. So many people go out as I have recommended and buy a couple of pigs for fattening only to change their minds a few months down the road. A typical phone call goes: 'We've decided to keep Flossie and breed from her because she's so lovely. How can we get her registered pedigree?' As the recipient of such calls, I can tell you it could drive you to drink!

An experienced pedigree breeder should be able to judge which pigs are good enough to breed from. The fact that your pig was sold for fattening means that it wasn't good enough. With all respect, your judgement of quality is based on the pig's temperament, his or her cuteness, the number of spots it has, the curliness of its tail or a hundred other perfectly logical (to you) reasons which have nothing to do with the pig's suitability to pass on its genes and hereditary characteristics to future generations.

So my very strong advice is – think it through before you commit to buying. You may well get very attached to one or more of the pigs you are fattening. If you think you might change from fattening for meat to breeding pedigree stock, then buy good-quality pedigree animals at the start. The key is to think ahead!

PIGS FOR BREEDING

*If you've just opened the book at this page,
then I'm afraid you need to go back and read the
preceding chapters – much of the information
in those pages applies here too. This section of
the book contains the 'extra' information you
will need in order to start a breeding herd,
however small.*

Pigs for breeding are that much bigger and need more space than just a few pigs kept for fattening but, again, as long as they have room to exercise and to get away from adverse weather, then the space requirement need not be huge. Some people will allow a pig to farrow in an ark but I would prefer to see a pig brought into a stable, loosebox or similar to make her nest and give birth. Pigs are usually the easiest of farm stock at this time with few complications. If complications do arise, you don't want to be scrabbling about on your hands and knees in an ark with a large sow who's suddenly become very grumpy, trying to turn a breeched birth. So plan your maternity wing accordingly.

THE MATERNITY WARD

This is my ideal farrowing house. Get as close to it as you can and you won't go far wrong (see the colour section for illustration). Start with a stable or loosebox with a split stable door. I'm assuming something about 3.6–4.6m (12–15ft) square. Partially divide the floor area with a low breezeblock wall 1–1.2m (3–4ft) high, leaving a gap of about 1.2m (4ft) at one end. Make sure that the outer door and the gap are not in line to minimise draughts. The floor should be solid concrete or similar. If you are re-flooring, line the base with egg trays before laying the final layer of cement on the top. This will trap air and help insulate the floor. In the outer area closest to the stable door, incorporate a drain to help keep the floor dry. To make life simple, plumb in a water supply ending in an automatic drinker about 23–30cm (9–12in) from the floor. (I did say this was my optimum farrowing pen!)

The outer area will be where the sow drinks, eats and dungs. The inner area will be a snug nursery. In one corner of the inner area, build a creep area for the little pigs, which is a warm place where the piglets can go when the sow is feeding or exercising. The sow should not be able to fit inside, so piglets within the creep are safe from being laid on. The creep should be about 1.2m (4ft) square and consist of two walls built out from the outer walls to form a 'box', but without a top. Leave out one breeze block from the lowest layer to form an entrance/exit for the piglets. Again it should be 1–1.2m (3–4ft) high. You should have the means to suspend a heat lamp over the creep. Around the walls of the stable, firmly fix a run of scaffolding poles using brackets so that they are 15–20cm (6–8in) above the floor and the same distance from the wall. A sow is large and clumsy in getting down and the pipes will act as an escape area if any little pigs are underneath her when she lies down.

Finally, old stables often have high ceilings, so for extra snugness, build a false ceiling that just allows you to stand up easily. Make it out of light boarding and heap loose straw on top for insulation. In hot weather, you can help keep things cool by leaving open the top of the stable door. Install a light

– an electric bulkhead fitting on the wall or ceiling is ideal – for when you need to attend a birth, which mostly tend to happen at night.

A sow does not need to be brought into her farrowing pen until 7–10 days before she's due and can be running outside with other pigs of a similar age up to that point. Make sure the farrowing quarters have been cleaned and disinfected since the last occupant and supply plenty of clean straw.

SELECTING PIGS FOR BREEDING

Now that we've got the farrowing quarters sorted out, let's go back to selecting the pigs. This is very different from choosing pigs for fattening. Firstly, while you can buy pigs at the same age – when they've just been weaned – you should also consider older gilts, say around six or seven months old, so that you can get used to them in the three or four months before they go to the boar. You could even buy gilts that are already 'in pig' and due to farrow in the next month or so.

The second point that I urge upon you is to consider only pure-bred, pedigree-registered pigs to breed from. Yes, most pigs in the UK are hybrids but they are highly selected, finely tuned creatures – like porcine Formula One cars – that are designed for a function and that function is the commercial meat market. You're not in that game or, if you are, you're reading the wrong book.

Choosing a Large Black x Berkshire gilt, which you then mate to a Tamworth will produce a lot of pretty pigs but their only function will be meat. They can never be a pedigree and the chances of you selling them to somebody else to breed from are remote. You would only be able to describe the meat as Free Range or Organic (provided you are registered with an appropriate authority), not by the breed name – more details on this are included in the chapter on Selling Meat (see page 74). Even if your main aim is to breed pigs for meat, selling some pedigree pigs at better-than-meat prices is beneficial to your profitability and your ego – the very best examples that you breed can be sold for pedigree breeding and will realise higher prices than meat animals.

As with meat pigs, go for the breed that you like: if you're persuaded to buy another, you'll always have a nagging feeling that you should have stuck to your first choice. Before you start looking at any pigs for sale, go to the British Pig Association (BPA) website (or the British Lop Pig Society website) and study the Standard of Excellence for your chosen breed. Within that are all the things you should look for before choosing your breeding stock. Don't get too bogged down with expressions such as 'spring of rib' or 'heavy jowl' – a feature that I defy anyone to identify in a young pig – but look instead at the teats (often described as 'the underline'), which are important in both the male and female because they are heritable. Not only must the minimum number be there (the more, the better), but they need to be evenly spaced and not 'inverted' or 'blind' or the newly born piglets won't be able to feed properly.

Legs are another important factor. They should be strong and the pig should stand well up on its pasterns (the part between the fetlock and the hoof). Look at the feet: it should seem as if the pig is almost standing on tiptoe with the 'hooves' having most ground contact. If the back part of the foot is the bit mainly in contact with the ground, the legs will let the pig down before too long and she won't breed and rear the numbers she should. The pig's back should be long and straight, not dipping behind the shoulders. The pig should have a broad loin (the area between the hips and shoulders) and good hams (the rounded thighs of the back legs).

Now use the Standard of Excellence to look at the breed points. Colour, shape of head, set of the ears and so on are important factors. If your chosen pig isn't up to standard here, her offspring are likely to fail too. A prick-eared British Saddleback or a white British Lop with faint signs of black spots are not good examples – avoid them. As with meat pigs, always go for healthy-looking specimens. Leave the runt or the sickly one for someone else.

For breeding stock, you might like to consider buying at a pedigree sale – these usually take place in the autumn across the country. The benefit of the sale is that you can compare and contrast and talk to the owners of a number of different pigs. Most such events will be preceded by a show. Alternatively, the stock forward (entrants) may be card-graded – where the animals are judged by a panel of experts and graded by card colour according to their qualities as a breeding animal – to give the buyer an independent assessment of the pig's good and not-so-good points. If the pig you fancy didn't do well in the show or was graded poorly and you cannot see why, ask someone. The owner will give you an opinion but it may be a touch biased so seek out the event's organisers or the judge or card grader and ask them. As with any auction, set an upper limit for each animal you

Mucking-out equipment

Weatherproof shelter or ark

Berkshire

British Lop

British Saddleback

Gloucestershire Old Spots

Large Black

Middle White

Oxford Sandy & Black

Tamworth

Large White

Welsh

British Landrace

Duroc

Hampshire

Kune Kune

Mangalitza

Pietrain

Vietnamese Pot Belly

Iron Age

Wild Boar

Corral

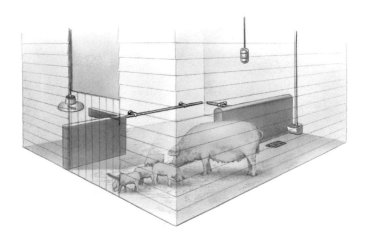

Farrowing house

intend to bid for and stick to it. The fleeting fame of appearing in *Farmers Weekly* for setting a new record price has to be offset against your arrival home and the response you give your spouse in answer to the query, 'How did it go?'

REPRODUCTION

Now you have the beginnings of your herd, the females that will turn into your sows. Assuming you didn't buy only in-pig gilts, we must turn to the mating process.

THE MATING GAME

Female pigs start coming on heat at around six months old but are not large enough to consider mating then. They should be big enough at around nine or ten months. Don't leave them a lot longer on the basis that they will be bigger still; porcine female fertility is a fickle thing and a breeding gilt or sow left 'empty' for too long becomes a problem pig.

Pigs come into heat every three weeks and it lasts around three days or so. Observation of the nether regions should reveal the vulva becoming enlarged with a little reddening (not so easy to see on black pigs). You may notice a change in temperament, with the pig becoming excitable and squealing more. If you apply your spread hands to her back, between her hips and her shoulders and press down, and if she stands without trying to escape, she's ready for mating.

Now you may feel that having brought you to this point, I should have first talked you through buying a boar. Well, not necessarily. It's generally reckoned not to be financially viable to keep and feed a boar with fewer than six females in his harem. And, if he's not kept busy in the reproductive department, he can become lazy and go off the idea, which makes him even more of a liability. In the world of rare breeds, there are often boars available to hire. Again check with the breed clubs or on their websites.

Sometimes you take the gilt or sow to the boar's home and leave her there on a B&B basis for at least three weeks. After mating, the farmer can check whether she comes on heat again in the next cycle and, if so, the boar can have a second go. This saves carting her to and fro. Some boars are available on a 'have wheels, will travel' basis and may be delivered to your holding to perform there. If this happens, don't just introduce him straight into his intended's boudoir: if she's not fully on heat, she's likely to attack him, which is not the best start to any courtship. Much better to put him in an empty pen and bring her to him. Remember too with all this travelling that Animal Movement Licences are required every time; your Movement Records Book must be completed and you will be subject to a 20 day standstill (except for stock going direct to an abattoir), after each movement (see page 9 for more information).

Two things to bear in mind about this boar. Firstly, make sure he's neither too big nor too small. If you've got a nine-month-old maiden gilt, she's in physical danger from being mated to a fully grown adult boar simply due to his weight and size. Secondly, 'your boar is half your herd' as the old expression goes; before you commit to any boar, compare him against the breed's Standard of Excellence. There's no point in being super critical in selecting your females only to use the first scrawny old boar that comes along. There will be a stud fee to pay to the boar's owner and if he's looking after your gilt for three weeks or more, there's her keep on top.

If you watch pigs mating, you will be aware that after a brief courtship – usually consisting of the boar sniffing her under her tail and pushing her flanks with his snout while he froths at the mouth – he eventually mounts her. Make sure his penis enters the right orifice – you may need to give a helping hand here. Following a brief period of activity, the boar will rest in position and remain there for quite some time. This is quite normal and you shouldn't interfere. Don't forget, he is attempting to fertilise a multiple birth and nature dictates the length of proceedings. Normally, they will mate again after several hours rest and may repeat the process the following day before she goes off heat.

ARTIFICIAL INSEMINATION

Then there's AI or artificial insemination. At the time of writing, AI is available for all rare breeds on a regular basis so it's something to consider, but there's certainly a knack to administering it and it may not suit you to begin with. However, if you can master AI and get pigs successfully impregnated, then it's cheap and convenient – the arrival of fresh boar semen in the caring hands of the postman won't shut you down for 20 days. Please note that the postman is just there to deliver it to you – he or she should not be expected to assist in the actual impregnation.

The way it works is like this. At the first sign of your female coming on heat, get on the phone and order your semen (see

Useful Addresses, see page 92). For some of the breeds, there's a choice of more than one boar so check out his details and look at his pedigree on the BPA website to get the best match with your female(s) (the British Lop equivalent is a phone call to the secretary). The obvious thing to look for first is that there are no common ancestors in the last four generations. That doesn't mean that just because you have a 'Josephine' gilt, the boar shouldn't have any 'Josephines' in his ancestry. But if your gilt's grandmother (grand-dam) was 'Bloggsfarm Josephine 10th' and the boar's mother (dam) was 'Bloggsfarm Josephine 10th', ie the same pig, then it would be wiser to find a different boar – at least until you've mastered the intricacies of line-breeding. (Line-breeding is the process of breeding closely related animals to 'fix' a particular attribute and should not be practised by amateurs as it can easily emphasise serious faults).

The semen – usually three 'straws' or phials – will be sent the same day by overnight delivery. This service is not guaranteed over the weekend so if you order on Friday, it may not arrive until Monday. Whenever it arrives, *do not put it in the fridge*. Keep it at room temperature. You should use it straight away providing your gilt is standing to the pressure test described earlier (see page 37). If she is, give her one straw in the morning, another that same evening and the third the following morning.

The three doses should come supplied with plastic catheters to get the semen right into the cervix. Most of these have a corkscrew thread on the end that mirrors the shape of the boar's penis and on reaching the cervix must be gently screwed anti-clockwise into the cervix until it locks into place.

The semen is fresh and if for some reason you mis-time your gilt being on heat, tip it down the drain. It won't last a further three weeks and it is not possible to extend its life through refrigerating or freezing it. Use it now or never.

Ask the AI station for written instructions on the use of AI and follow them carefully. Two aspects to point out: firstly, when inserting the catheter into the vagina, angle it slightly upwards (at about 30 degrees) to avoid the bladder. Secondly, once everything's in place, be patient! The semen must flow into the catheter at its own pace; it's a long, slow process and cannot be hurried so don't squeeze the bottle and try to rush things. The boar doesn't!

Whether you relied on a boar or the postman, keep a careful eye on your gilt three weeks hence because if she shows signs of coming on heat again then you will need to repeat the process from beginning to end.

GIVING BIRTH

Gestation takes three months, three weeks and three days or between 111 and 116 days in total. In times past, before the availability of printed calendars, Danish pig farmers were said to cut a small notch at the base of their thumbnail when the mating took place and by the time the notch grew out at the top of the nail, farrowing was due. I've never tried it myself.

The gilt or sow can continue to mix with her peers while in-pig but should be separated and moved to her farrowing quarters around seven to ten days before she is due. At this time give her a dose of a combined wormer and parasite control so that if she does have lice or intestinal worms, she doesn't pass them on to her litter. Ask your vet's advice on which product to use and buy it from the vet or via the internet. Details of how much you should be feeding at this time, during farrowing and while she is suckling her litter are given later in the chapter.

Given plenty of straw, the gilt or sow will make her nest, get herself comfortable and prepare for the big event. It's important not to overdo the straw as little pigs can get lost and squashed under mountains of the stuff. There should be enough to make a decent bed with no floor showing through, and it should be relatively flat after she's made her nest. If you think she's close to giving birth, when she's lying down, gently rub the udder with your open hand and then squeeze on her teats between your thumb and forefinger. If a drop of milk appears, she should farrow in the next 24 hours.

Some gilts and sows are perfectly amenable and friendly towards you until it comes to farrowing time. If your pig shows signs of being unhappy at your presence, respect her wishes and leave her to it by retreating away until she is content again. Hopefully, you will still be in a position to observe proceedings. Pigs, unlike cattle and sheep, rarely have complications during birth – it has been described as being similar to shelling peas – but issues do sometimes arise and you need to be ready to help. If a pig has started giving birth and seems to be struggling, with nothing else happening for 30 minutes or more, there may be a problem with two pigs trying to come out at once or a pig presenting itself in such a way as to be blocking the birth canal – in which case it's time to get the vet to lend a helping hand (and arm).

I use the term 'lend' loosely here as vets are never cheap. Most vets nowadays specialise in small animal care, which means that the small animals conveniently come to them during surgery hours, pay on the nail and everything's hunky dory. The days of turning out in the middle of the night to a cow with calving complications in a muddy field in a howling storm are nothing more than a nightmare to most vets today. So ask around the local farming community; they will know which vets are good with farm stock.

Involving a vet in a farrowing should be the exception, not the rule, and your gilt should produce her piglets over a period of between two and six hours. There may be a brief interlude halfway through when she gets up and moves around before getting back to business. The end of the farrowing is indicated by the release of the afterbirth, which all but fills a bucket. Check with your local Animal Health Office for guidance on disposing of animal by-products – contact details are listed in *A Guide for New Keepers: Pigs* (see Further Reading, page 93).

THE PIGLETS

How many piglets will she have in a litter? Well, the world record for a pig is 37 but for a rare breed gilt, the more normal range is 8–12 but it may be fewer or more. If the latter, then you can begin to appreciate the

need for a good underline of well-placed teats. Incidentally, you will observe that the strongest piglets utilise the most forward teats, which is where most milk will be found. The smaller, weaker siblings must argue over the hindmost teats, which are a little less prolific. It's called survival of the fittest.

Put an infra-red lamp above the creep as an alternative place for the piglets to sleep. You will have to judge the height carefully. Too low and you're in danger of cooking them, too high and they won't feel the benefit. If it is on and the piglets are scattered on the straw below the lamp rather than huddled together, it's too hot and needs raising. In cold weather, you should keep the lamp on until the pigs are a week old. Even during the summer, bear in mind how chilly it can get at night and switch it on then if not during the day.

Some gilts can be shocked or frightened by the first appearance of a piglet and attack it. There they are, having been getting bigger and bigger over the past few months and now feeling decidedly strange, when along comes this unfamiliar little creature and it all gets too much. If this happens and she kills a piglet, don't panic. Get in there and as each new piglet is born, lift it carefully and place it in a cardboard box lined with hay for warmth, with its siblings. Once farrowing is complete, give her a Guinness mash consisting of about three or four pints with a pound of meal stirred in. This should send her to sleep without interfering with her letting her milk down, which some drugs can do. Once she's asleep, place the piglets at the udder and let them get on with it. It is very unlikely she will attack any more once she wakes up again.

At a normal birth, you will observe each little piglet being born and freeing itself of the placenta. If it struggles, you can give it a hand. It will also break the umbilical cord as instinct guides it away from the rear of its mother – where a brother or sister may land on its head if it hangs around – and round to the milk bar of bloated teats awaiting it. Like all newborns, it will nudge the teat before suckling. If it doesn't seem to get the message that the teat is the source of nutrition, you can gently lift it onto a teat until it gets going.

Once it fills its little belly, it will go away from the nest to find a suitable area to relieve its bladder, an instinct that is not shared by other domestic creatures, which will pee and dung wherever they happen to be. And they call pigs dirty!

It is essential that the sow has ready access to clean, fresh water and plenty of it. Just in case you didn't manage to install an automatic drinker in the farrowing pen, make sure you keep the water bowl well topped-up during and after farrowing. In order to produce the milk to feed so many hungry mouths, she will need gallons of the stuff.

Little pigs require a dose of iron otherwise they can suffer from anaemia and die. In commercial units they will either give this in injectable form in the first few days of life or via an oral paste. Both are effective although the latter will be more suited to the type of pig keeper we are addressing here. However, this iron can be obtained from the soil and until the piglets go out, you can counteract the problem much more cheaply by providing a sod of soil placed in the pen or creep area. What is more, the playful piglets will have great fun breaking up the turf and playing with the soil. Just make sure that when you cut the sod, you don't take it from an existing piggy area where it may be the source of intestinal worms.

SURVIVAL OF THE FITTEST

In almost every litter there will be one or maybe two runts, pigs that are small and feeble compared with their siblings. They may not survive beyond a few days, which can be distressing to the new pig-keeper but is nature's way. Be aware that fostering such a piglet can be hugely demanding on time and effort: it will require feeding every couple of hours, day and night, and will never make a thriving, well-grown pig. Even with farrowing rails installed, you may get the occasional 'accident', especially in the first few days, when the sow squashes a piglet as she gets down. Sod's Law usually dictates that this was the biggest/healthiest/best in the litter but, hey-ho, such is life (and death). Check with your local Animal Health Office for guidance on disposing of any dead piglets (animal by-products) – contact details are listed in *A Guide for New Keepers: Pigs* (see Further Reading, page 93).

From a few hours old, the piglets will be full of fun and spend waking hours alternately feeding and playing. Piglets are very advanced compared with puppies and kittens, which are born with their eyes closed, and unless the weather is very cold or wet, the sow and her piglets can be let out for some exercise every day after the first 48 hours. However, don't leave them out all the time until they reach 10 or 14 days.

Watch out for cuts on the faces of some of the piglets or on the sow's udder. Left unchecked, her teats will become sore and she will be reluctant to feed her family. This is usually a sign of one or more dominant boar pigs using their newly found tusks as weapons to dominate their siblings. If you pick up the bully boys and gently open their mouths, you will see that the two incisors on the bottom jaw are growing outwards as mini tusks. It is quite easy to snip off the tusks at the bend with a pair of nail clippers. This does not hurt the little boar unduly and he will return to the family less able to bully or damage the udder. However, you should only do this if the tusks are causing a problem (it is routine in some commercial establishments, as is tail docking, which should never be necessary in an extensive system – the sort of set-up we are talking about here).

HOW TO PICK UP A PIGLET

Picking small pigs up needs to be done carefully as they will squeal loudly and the sow's reaction will be instantaneous, fast, loud and frightening – so make sure you cannot be cornered by her. The best way is to pick the small pig up gently by one or both of its hind legs as this causes least consternation. Move outside the pen and close the door before lifting him up and inspecting his teeth or doing anything else to him. Once you return the patient to the sow, she will cluck round him to make sure he is all right before going back to doing what she was doing before.

FEEDING PIGS FOR BREEDING

As you will have gathered, I favour our rare and traditional breeds over the more commercial types and I believe it is essential for them to have a balanced diet that reflects their needs. Just because they were treated as scavengers and fed as such in historic times, does not mean that you can do this today and produce healthy breeding stock or well-finished meat animals. I will also reiterate here, because it is so important, that it is illegal to feed pigs on anything that has been in a commercial or domestic kitchen and certainly never anything that contains, or may have come into contact with, meat or meat products of any sort.

FEEDING ADULT BREEDING STOCK

Outdoor adult sows need to be kept in good condition for breeding purposes. Good condition in this respect largely means not too fat. Lean is beautiful as far as successful breeding goes, but not excessively so.

Once the piglets are weaned, top priority is to dry up the sow's milk supply quickly: for the first 24 hours cut out food and give only the barest amount of water. Next day give her just 1kg (2lb) of food and a little more water, gradually increasing over the next three to four days to 3.5kg (8lb) of food and plenty of water. After this cut the food back to around 2.25kg (5lb) for the next three weeks. In the first two months or so after mating, the outdoor sow can be kept in condition on as little as 1.3–1.8kg (3–4lb) a day. Once she's in-pig, if she's outdoors with plenty of grass and rooting, she should need only 1.3–1.5kg (3–3½lb) of feed a day but a bit more if supplementary rations are scarce.

If you are giving adult pigs additional feeds such as potatoes or sugar beet or fodder beet, the late 'grandfather' of Gloucestershire Old Spots, breeder George Styles, recommended putting an old lorry or tractor tyre flat on the ground and placing the roots inside. The sows will enjoy the challenge of getting to the food and benefit accordingly.

In the two weeks before farrowing is due, you can start feeding another 0.5kg (1lb) or so more food a day but cut it back again two to three days before the event. Watch out for the sow becoming constipated – a dangerous state pre-farrowing. If she does, mix together a couple of double handfuls of bran with enough hot water to make a paste and stir in 2–3 tablespoons of molasses. Let it cool and add this to her usual feed; it should unblock things before farrowing starts. Repeat if necessary.

Once she has farrowed, for the first 24 hours give her feed only if she wants it, but make sure she always has a plentiful supply of clean water. Thereafter, calculate her feed while she's suckling at 1.3–1.8kg (3–4lb) plus 0.5kg (1lb) for every piglet she is feeding. So for a litter of 10, that's 6kg (13–14lb) of grub a day.

Remember, this is a guideline, not an instruction. Pigs vary in their constitution just as humans do and you may need to adjust the amounts accordingly. The important thing is the condition of the pig, which shouldn't be too fat or too thin.

In the chapter on Pigs for Meat (see page 14), we looked at the various forms of pig feed in terms of meal, pellets or cobs, and the same comments apply for breeding stock. Again, 16–18% protein should be the target. Store the feed carefully in a dry area where rodents cannot get access to it. If it gets damp and mouldy, throw it away. It may make the pigs ill.

The breeding boar should be fed on the roughly the same regime as a sow in the early phase of pregnancy. Adjust the amount to ensure he doesn't get too fat.

WEANING PIGLETS

You can wean the pigs at any time from three to eight weeks, although most rare-breed keepers will opt for the latter as this makes best use of the mothering ability of the dam (the pedigree mother) and the ready supply of nutritious milk she is producing. You can supplement the milk at around three weeks of age by feeding creep feed (a specially formulated feed that includes milk powder). To avoid the sow hoovering this up, put it in a dish in the creep area where only the little pigs can gain access. Never leave stale creep feed in the dish and discard any leftovers before topping it up with fresh.

If you don't give them creep feed, you may well notice the inquisitive little pigs 'sharing' mother's rations from about this age, which shouldn't do them any harm and minimises stress in the change of diet when they are weaned.

Three weeks after farrowing, the sow will come on heat again but should not be put to the boar until the piglets are weaned. However, the heat will usually cause scouring in the piglets for a day or two – this is quite normal and does not require any treatment providing it lasts no longer than a couple of days.

ONCE PIGS ARE WEANED

How much you feed pigs from weaning upwards will vary, depending upon the method of husbandry. The reason for this is simple. Pigs with access to fresh air will eat grass, although its nutritional value to them is much lower than for other farm stock: remember, the pig's digestive system is much closer to our own and the pig has similar dentition and only one stomach. Pigs outside will also root using their strong snouts to turn up the earth. In the process, they will consume insects and grubs, roots and other bits and pieces. So in theory, the outdoor pig needs a little less food provided. However, on the other hand, the outdoor pig is burning off more calories in the process and building more muscle, so shouldn't be short changed either!

I have already said that pigs from weaning up to 40kg (88lb) in weight can be fed *ad lib* without detriment on a 16–18% protein proprietary feed. However, if you don't have the means to feed young pigs this way, as a rule of thumb, you should calculate for around 0.5kg (1lb) of feed a day for every month of age. Therefore, at weaning at eight weeks, they should have 1kg (2lb) a day; at 12 weeks, 1.3kg (3lb); at 16 weeks, 1.8kg (4lb) and so on. At 20 weeks, level off at 2.25kg (5lb) a day and hold it there until the pigs are ready for slaughter.

Experience is the best guide. If, at slaughter, your pigs are excessively fat, then cut back on these quantities a bit or at least review what supplements they might be getting either direct from the ground or from your garden. It's easy for the first-time pig keeper to spoil their animals, literally. Pigs are, like dogs, descended from scavengers and will also overeat given the chance. This is due to their ancestors consuming whatever was available and wasting nothing lest tomorrow's searching be in vain.

Outdoor pigs can be susceptible to being poisoned by certain plants although, generally speaking, pigs are quite sensible about what they eat and what they reject. Plants such as yew, foxglove, ragwort, monk's hood or wolf's bane and hemlock are all potentially lethal to pigs. Bracken is carcinogenic and its effects can build up over time – it can eventually prove deadly after continued exposure. Potatoes are considered a good supplementary feed by many pig keepers but green potatoes that have been exposed to daylight should be avoided, as should rotten or very old sprouting potatoes. When feeding 'extras' to pigs, just ask yourself if you'd be prepared to eat the food. If not, don't give it to the pigs either!

PEDIGREE PIGS

You will recall that my earlier advice was to buy and breed from good-quality pedigree pigs, but the pedigree will only be transferable to your piglets if you follow the procedure to become a pedigree breeder yourself.

REGISTERING YOUR STOCK

For most breeds, you will need to join the British Pig Association (BPA); if you have chosen British Lops then join the British Lop Pig Society (BLPS). The first thing to do is to register a prefix – your official herd name – by which all your registered stock will be known. Having ensured that both your gilt and the boar used were registered pedigree, the next stage is to birth notify your litter.

If one or both of the parents of your litter was not fully registered but only birth notified, that should not be a major problem but you should get the pig(s) concerned registered by the breeder(s) before the farrowing takes place. There is a fee for this, which you should expect to pay, and the pig concerned will now have an official pedigree name. This consists of the breeder's herd prefix, for example, 'Stanner'; the pig's bloodline name, for example, 'Lottie'; followed by a number which is either the xth pig of that family registered in the herd (for example, Stanner Lottie 4th), or will be the ear number (see below) of that pig – for example, Stanner Lottie 52nd, where Lottie is the 52nd pig birth notified in that herd.

Birth notification can be done online with the BPA or by a paper form with both organisations. The form is simple to complete and I recommend that you birth notify every piglet, even if none are suitable for registration. This is because, once notified and earmarked (see below), they are traceable back to you and, with pigs notified to the BPA, you can download a certificate guaranteeing their breeding – which is useful when selling meat from such pigs.

MARKING YOUR PIGS

Part of the birth notification process is to mark the pigs' ears permanently. In white, spotted and ginger-red breeds this is done by tattooing a number in the ear; for black breeds it is by notching a sort of semaphore code to identify them. Both processes are bloody and distressing until you get used to them, but necessary for identification. I strongly urge that for your first litter, you find someone who has done it before to show you how to carry out the operation (tattooing does not involve visiting a parlour in the seedy part of town). It is best to get your own equipment: for tattooing this can cost anything up to a couple of hundred pounds but it should last a lifetime. The notching process is simpler and the notching pliers much cheaper, but you need to be very precise where you cut the notches or the numbers won't be clear. There are different systems for different breeds – you can see the British Saddleback's system on their website. Berkshires and Large Blacks share a different numbering system, which the BPA will advise you about – don't get them muddled up!

Earmarking must be carried out by eight weeks of age or before the piglets are mixed with other pigs. You will need an assistant. In practice, lifting a struggling pig at nearly eight weeks old is hard work so I recommend you do the task at 16–21 days old when the piglets are still light enough to handle easily. Because of the sow's maternal instincts when she hears a squeal, you need to get her out of the way first. I suggest you let her out of the pen but close the door on the piglets. Get them all in the creep area, then block off the entrance so that you can reach in and pick out one at a time. Once everything's been done to him or her, put him or her down in the main pen area so that you're not picking up the same pig more than once. Again, lift by one or both hind legs and hold the pig firmly in your arm.

Firstly inspect the piglet carefully. Count and record the number of teats (on little boars as well). If a boar pig, has it got two testicles descended? Are there any visible hernias or other obvious defects? Next check for breed points such as broken saddles (in Saddlebacks), colouring and markings or roses in the coat and note these also. Tattoo or notch each pig with a consecutive number according to the Birth Notification form. Note for yourself any pigs that you have not found faults with, which may be ones that could be registered at a later date. Both earmarking processes are bloody, but rub a little antiseptic into the wounds and it's surprising how quickly they heal. Once the creep is empty and pigs have been inspected and earmarked, you can let the sow back in. Again she will be agitated for a moment or two until she has inspected her brood but then will settle down as if nothing had happened.

SEPARATING THE LITTER

You will notice that, as the piglets get bigger and more boisterous, the sow becomes less interested in them and, at around eight weeks, she seems to indicate that she's had enough of them. At whatever age you wean them, move the sow away from the piglets, never vice versa. The sow should now go back to the boar straight away. This is not industrialised farming but vital animal husbandry: a sow left 'empty' for any unnecessary period will become a lot harder to get into pig again and may even become barren. The only exception is if she has reared a large and demanding litter and is now particularly thin, in which case she may need feeding up for a couple of weeks to put some (but not too much), condition back on her.

After separation, the piglets can be moved to their own pen or run and you can thoroughly clean and disinfect the farrowing pen pending the next occupant's arrival. The piglets can now be sold, fattened or run on (kept within the herd) if good enough for registration and breeding to expand your herd.

The accommodation for the litter should be out of sight and earshot of the sow if at all possible. If you have a stock boar – assuming that by now you have enough breeding females to justify one – remember that by keeping your gilts, you may soon render him redundant because you won't want him mating his own daughters.

YOUR NEW-FOUND RESPONSIBILITY

Congratulations! If you've followed my advice so far, you are now a breeder of pedigree pigs. Your details will appear in the herd book of your chosen breed and breeders in future generations will look back at them and wonder who you were and what your pigs were like.

This brings new responsibilities. Not just those of good husbandry, ensuring the welfare and well-being of your stock at all times. No, I'm talking about the responsibilities of maintaining the gene pool of the breed in the very best order. Because these are rare breeds, the gene pool is tiny and even if your herd is small, you can greatly influence the future viability of the breed – even if you don't fully appreciate it.

Every pig that you register and breed from or sell for others to breed from will affect future generations. If you are lazy, ignorant of the Standards of Excellence or out to make a quick buck, you can do untold damage to your chosen breed.

So please, don't be the name in a herd book that future generations of pig keepers remember as being 'the breeder who nearly wrecked the breed'. Do the job properly. Be rigorous in selection; reject anything less than perfect; talk to those more experienced for help and guidance; complete and maintain your pedigree records promptly, accurately and perfectly. If you're not sure which boar is the sire of a litter, *don't even birth notify them* – we've moved on here to a larger operation where there's more than one boar on site! If two litters have become mixed before you've earmarked and recorded them and the sows are cross-suckling them, *don't birth notify them*. You don't know for sure which sow is the dam of which pigs. And if they're not birth notified, you can't be tempted to register them.

Talking of temptation, once you start selling pigs for fattening, you will soon be contacted by someone asking you to register one of those pigs because the buyer has changed his or her mind and now wants to breed from her (or even him). *Please don't*. You made a carefully informed judgement that that pig was not good enough to breed from. You used your growing awareness of what is or what is not good pedigree breeding stock. That pig will not have changed. Those poorly placed teats won't have moved. The blind ones won't suddenly have come good. Those bow legs won't miraculously have disappeared. That dip behind the shoulders won't have straightened out.

That pig wasn't good enough to breed from then and it won't have changed since. Be resolute and say 'no' as firmly as you can. Back it up by writing or emailing the BPA and informing them that the pig in question (give the earmark number), is not to be registered if the owner tries to go behind your back.

As in most walks of life, there are cowboys out there already. Don't be another one.

THE BREEDS

*Having read this far, you will know by now that
I am strongly in favour of horses for courses and that the
old-fashioned rare breeds are ideally suited to the type of
management described so far. But just in case you are not
convinced, we'll have a look at all the breeds available in
the UK and I'll try to describe them for you.*

RARE AND TRADITIONAL BREEDS

BERKSHIRE

The Berkshire is a delightful breed that will suit many
operations. Technically, it is the oldest British breed because
pedigree recording for it began marginally earlier than for the
other breeds in the 1880s. The Berkshire is not the largest
of breeds and is a specialist pork producer, maturing early
with the need to slaughter for pork at slightly lighter weights
than most others – around 65–70kg (145–155lb). I would
recommend it. Among notable keepers of the breed in times
past have been Queen Victoria and Beatrix Potter. The
Berkshire is officially listed as a rare breed and has its
own breeders' club (see Useful Addresses, page 90).

DESCRIPTION: It appears to be black but is really a deep
brown colour with white points on all four feet, the tail
tip and a blaze on the face. It is prick-eared and lively and
one of the most glamorous of breeds. See colour section
for illustration.

BRITISH LOP

The British Lop is probably our rarest pig breed with least reason to be so except that it doesn't look rare. The Lop, which used to be known as the National Long White Lop-Eared Breed, originated around Tavistock in the area where Devon and Cornwall meet and remained for many decades a well-kept secret as a local West-Country breed. I would thoroughly recommend the British Lop for anyone looking to fatten pigs or begin pedigree breeding. It is the only indigenous breed still to have its own dedicated breed society (see Useful Addresses, page 90).

DESCRIPTION: The Lop is docile and makes an excellent mother. It has a top-quality carcase for either pork or bacon. It is a white breed with lop ears (see below and colour section for illustration) and to the uninitiated can look similar to the Welsh and Landrace. Unfortunately, because it is not coloured or spotted and doesn't have any distinctive features such as a squashed snout, the majority of hobby farmers and smallholders who have done so much to help conserve rare breeds have snubbed it.

The British Saddleback originated in 1967 through a clumsy attempt at conservation before the advent of the Rare Breeds Survival Trust (RBST). There were two breeds with similar markings, but no evidence of any closer relationship: the Wessex Saddleback and the Essex. The Wessex, which originated around the Isle of Purbeck where Dorset and Hampshire meet, was then a mainstream breed. But the Essex, generally reckoned to be the gentleman's pig – as opposed to the Wessex, the farmer's pig – was in trouble and the affairs of the breed society had just been taken over by the National Pig Breeders Association (NPBA, later to become the BPA). With declining numbers, the powers that be at the NPBA decided that, instead of recording the Essex in a separate herd book, it would be more convenient to amalgamate the two breeds and have just one herd book for the British Saddleback. The amalgamated breed declined in popularity until nearly all the significant Wessex herds had disappeared within a decade of the amalgamation and by 1979 the combined breed had slipped so far as to be recognised as a rare breed by the RBST.

You may be confused by some people who still refer to the Essex breed and some enthusiasts believe that there are pure Essex pigs still in existence. I was involved in the 1990s in collecting blood samples from all rare breeds for a DNA analysis of breeds from across Europe and deliberately targeted examples of both some of the claimed pure Essex, as well as some recent imports from Australia said to be pure Wessex Saddlebacks. The DNA results failed to identify the Essex as being anything different from the mainstream British Saddlebacks but the Australian Wessex were distinct. They were not kept pure in the UK and now form part of the wider

British Saddleback gene mix, but they are kept pure in Australia, albeit in tiny numbers. For more information visit the breeders' club website (see Useful Addresses, page 91).

DESCRIPTION: Both original breeds were lop-eared, black in colour with an unbroken saddle of white hair covering both front legs and going over the shoulders. The Essex also had white hind feet up to the hock, a white tail-tip and a white nose, and either colour combination is acceptable in the breed today (see colour section for illustration). Today's British Saddlebacks make excellent, docile mothers, are among the most prolific of breeds, are ideal for outdoor systems and also produce excellent quality pork and bacon.

GLOUCESTERSHIRE OLD SPOTS

The most successful of the rare breeds in terms of numbers, the Gloucestershire Old Spots or Orchard Pig would make an ideal candidate for anyone following this method of pig keeping. Docile and excellent breeding pigs, the Old Spots can and do produce the highest quality pork and bacon. This lop-eared breed originated around the banks of the river Severn in the Vale of Berkeley, between Gloucester and Bristol. Originally they were kept on the small dairy farms of the area to consume the skimmed milk and whey, and were turned out in the orchards in autumn to fatten on the windfall fruit. They count among their keepers and admirers HRH The Princess Royal, Elizabeth Hurley and bass-player Alex James. Further details can be found at the breeders' club website (see Useful Addresses, page 91).

DESCRIPTION: They are the oldest pedigree spotted breed in the world. Folklore has it that the spots began as bruises from falling fruit when the pigs were let loose in the orchard. The Breed Standard stipulates a minimum of one clearly defined spot but also prohibits excessive marking where, say, more than half the body is black in colour. The ears on an adult Gloucestershire Old Spots should just about cover the face, meeting at the snout (see colour section for illustration).

LARGE BLACK

Like the British Lop this breed originated in the West Country and in Germany they are still known as Cornwalls. Suited to both pork and bacon production, they need a little care to keep them lean but the meat is delicious. If the Large Black is your fancy, then go for it. More information is available from the breed website (see Useful Addresses, page 91).

DESCRIPTION: Black all over and with lop ears, these are the ideal outdoor breed as they will never suffer from sunburn. Bathed and oiled-up, these are the glamour-puss pigs of the showing world; when the sun glints off their shining skin they are certainly eye-catching (see colour section for illustration).

MIDDLE WHITE

The Middle White originated in Yorkshire from crossing
the Large White (see page 66) with the Small White, a fancy
breed that became extinct around 1912. The Small White had
been heavily influenced by oriental pigs imported on trading
vessels in the 18th and 19th centuries and used to improve
many of the old British breeds. It was these Far Eastern types
that imparted the squashed face. All British breeds are said
to carry some degree of such influence; the Middle White
the most and the Tamworth the least. The Middle White for
all its unusual appearance was the specialist pork producer
and up until the 1930s was the most populous breed in the
country. Government interference in the market meant that
the emphasis changed from pork to bacon production to
reduce dependence on Danish imports – a policy that left
the Middle White (and Berkshire), with nowhere to go
except down in numbers.

The Middle White for years was known as The London
Porker and in Japan its flesh was so highly regarded that
a shrine was built in its honour. The celebrity chef Antony
Worrall Thompson keeps them. More information is available
from the breed website (see Useful Addresses, page 91).

DESCRIPTION: The 'ugly' breed. The Middle White is
distinguished by its squashed snout – the porcine equivalent
of the British bulldog (see colour section for illustration). It
is ideal for the type of operation so far described except that
I would add a caveat that it is not quite as hardy as the other
rare breeds and may prefer to be in a spacious indoor pen in
the depths of winter rather than clambering about in the mud.

Oxford Sandy & Black
(Plum Pudding Pigs)

This is not a rare breed as recognised by the Rare Breeds Survival Trust, and it has a herd book dating back to only 1985. There is some evidence of a similar-looking pig in times past but no pedigree was recorded. In addition, if you cross almost any combination of Berkshire, Tamworth, Large Black and Gloucestershire Old Spots, you get pigs that, to all intents and purposes, look the same as these. However, that does not mean that pedigree Sandy & Blacks are not ideally suited to the management system I have described. The breeders' club can be contacted via their website (see Useful Addresses, page 91).

DESCRIPTION: The background colour ranges from a pale orange to a deep chestnut. The spots are more blotchy than the Gloucestershire Old Spots and there is sometimes a lot of black colour on the pigs. The ears are not full lop but are carried forward rather than covering the face (see colour section for illustration). The pigs are hardy and free from the danger of sunburn; the meat is truly delicious and the breed is docile.

Tamworth

There's probably no better sight than the sun shining on a ginger Tamworth's back highlighting the golden bristles, unless it's an autumn woodland scene with the yellows, golds and reds of broadleaf trees echoed by a group of snuffling Tammies. The prick-eared Tamworth is named after the Staffordshire town believed to be its place of origin. It is another hardy breed ideally suited to outdoor life and it, too, spurns sunburn. Originally kept for bacon production, it was cruelly cast aside with the arrival of the Nordic Landrace and is as good today for pork as bacon. The Tamworth breeders' club can be reached via their website (see Useful Addresses, page 91).

DESCRIPTION: A lively breed whose curiosity is not impaired by ears that cover the face (see colour section for illustration). Ginger with golden bristles, the Tamworth is descended from the old English forest pig and has minimal influence from the oriental pigs used in times past to improve British breeds. Thus the Tamworth's head is longer than all others, giving it a prodigious tool with which to dig.

MODERN BRITISH BREEDS

LARGE WHITE

The chances are that unless things change radically in the next few years, the Large White too will be listed as a 'rare' breed as numbers of pedigree pigs continue to decline. The reason for this is that most commercial pig production, as already mentioned, relies on highly developed hybrids that perform miracles of growth and produce huge volumes of lean meat. Because of the way the market is structured, commercial farmers have to rely on hybrid pigs: it's the only hope they have of being able to remain in business while supplying the supermarkets who control how much is paid for all forms of meat. Sadly, even with these hybrid superpigs, the supermarkets won't pay enough to cover the cost of production and soon most commercial production will be driven overseas where costs – and welfare standards – are lower. Almost all these hybrids use some element of Large Whites in their configuration but they don't need more than a few boars and artificial insemination to achieve this. Thus the pedigree animal that has been one of the most successful breeds in the world, is in sharp decline in its native country.

This breed, which has influenced commercial pig production worldwide, was developed not by one of the famous stock improvers of the 18th and 19th centuries, but by a mill worker and his wife who lived in a terraced cottage in Keighley in Yorkshire. Joseph Tuley kept pigs for what was called 'pig racing' in the early 19th century – which to you and me is pig showing. It was his hobby and he spent all his spare time and energy developing the ultimate type of pig that would win every show. He succeeded and the money he made allowed him to move to a detached house in a more affluent part of town as people flocked to him to buy the offspring of his newly developed Large White breed. The Large White is not ideal for the type of husbandry described in this book but would do at a pinch if you are desperate to keep the breed.

DESCRIPTION: Long bodied pigs with fine white hair. The head is quite long and the breed has pricked ears (see colour section for illustration). The breed has been changed in recent years to a longer, leaner type of animal yet to my old-fashioned eyes, the closest thing to a perfect pig is one of the deeper-bodied, long pigs seen widely in the post-war years when Large Whites really did rule the world.

WELSH

The Welsh pig is a conundrum. It is officially deemed to be rare due to the sharp decline in its numbers in recent times, although I tend to think of it still as a mainstream breed better suited to commercial situations. That's not to say that it doesn't have a place in smallholder operations, but its growth rate and lean carcase means that it does not perform in the same way as rare and traditional breeds (see pages 58–65). The Welsh has changed considerably over the last 30 years as breeders have tried to get it closer to the Landrace (see page 68). Unfortunately, breeder success has spelled their demise: the market found no need for both a Landrace and a look-alike, and numbers declined considerably.

DESCRIPTION: A white breed with lop ears, it can be difficult to tell apart from the Landrace or the British Lop, until you come to recognise the finer points of the breed, which mainly concern ear carriage (see colour section for illustration). It is an inherently good mother pig and is quite easy to keep.

IMPORTED BREEDS

BRITISH LANDRACE

Some would argue that the Landrace, having been resident in the UK for more than 50 years now, deserves to be recognised as a British breed. However, this most successful of commercial breeds was developed in Denmark in the early years of the 20th century specifically to target the UK's bacon requirements. Its development relied heavily on Large Whites imported from the best herd in Britain crossed with native Danish pigs and in many ways it fulfilled its brief.

DESCRIPTION: Crossing the two breeds produced this long, lean white pig with an extra rib – and thus more rashers per side (see colour section for illustration). The Landrace is temperamentally unsuited to small-scale operations. I would recommend that you leave it to the commercial pig producer.

DUROC

The Duroc, or more correctly, the Duroc Jersey, has been developed in America for commercial meat production. It has been imported and used in the UK to try to get intramuscular fat or marbling into commercial hybrids. It was developed in the US using pigs imported from Guinea in Africa and despite claims from some, there is no evidence that Tamworths featured in their make-up.

DESCRIPTION: This is a brown-coloured pig with strangely small ears (see colour section for illustration). The Duroc is a commercial breed imported to do a specific job and is not the ideal type for the sort of operation described here.

Hampshire

Another American breed although some supermarkets are
trying to claim that they are a 'traditional British breed'.
They were named Hampshire because they were based
on some pigs exported from a Hampshire port – probably
Southampton – in the 1820s but there is some evidence that
the pigs in question originally came from Scotland. Whatever
the true history, the fact that they share a colour-marking
gene with the British Saddleback does not necessarily
make them related.

DESCRIPTION: The Hampshire carries similar markings
to the British Saddleback although it has pricked ears and
a conformation totally at odds with the current Saddleback,
being lean with long legs typical of American pigs (see colour
section for illustration).

Kune Kune

A small breed imported in the 1990s from New Zealand
where its Maori name apparently means 'fat and round'.
They are very appealing, but unless you are thinking purely
in terms of pets, than you must consider what sort of carcase
you are looking for. Kune Kune take longer to reach a stage
when they become fit to slaughter – the carcase is quite a bit
smaller than our native breeds and there is a danger of them
being over-fat. However, these smaller pigs need less feed
so it may be that the Kune Kune meets your needs.

DESCRIPTION: It is the only pig breed (except the Vietnamese
Pot Belly, see page 71) that does not breed true for colour and
comes in a variety of different hues. Some of the pigs have

wattles hanging from the neck, but not all do. They are
prick-eared and cute (see colour section for illustration).

MANGALITZA

The Mangalitza was imported in recent years from Austria and
is widespread in eastern Europe. As a fairly unreconstructed
breed, they will produce a fattier carcase than our rare breeds
and with numbers still being fairly low over here, there is a
premium price being demanded for breeding stock. Unless
you have a yearning for a pig with a woolly coat and the
ability to produce lard, then this may not be the ideal breed
for you.

DESCRIPTION: The Mangalitza is unusual in having a
dense, woolly coat. This derives from a gene shared with
the extinct Lincolnshire Curly Coat but there the similarities
end – despite the fact that some breeders are trying to link
the two breeds more closely. It comes in several colours
although pigs in the UK are mainly blondes (see colour
section for illustration). The alternatives are either red or
swallow-bellied (brown or black with pale underparts).

PIETRAIN

A Belgian breed notable for a double-muscled rump,
thus producing more meat for the commercial farmer.
What it is about Belgium, I do not know but from this small
country have come double-muscled cattle (Belgian Blue) and
double-muscled sheep (Beltex), all of which to my mind, look
very unnatural – but then I'm not a commercial farmer.

DESCRIPTION: The Pietrain is a spotted breed with prick ears (see colour section for illustration). It has no place in the type of operation you are considering.

VIETNAMESE POT BELLY

Imported originally for laboratory work, they spread to zoos and subsequently beyond. It is difficult to make a case for keeping them for meat production because the carcase is small and over-fat. The market for so-called pet pigs seems to have declined and so I'm not sure there is any reason to justify breeding them, unless you simply hanker after them – especially as some can be temperamental.

DESCRIPTION: The Vietnamese is a small, short-legged breed. As the name implies, it is pot-bellied and on some adult pigs, the belly actual drags along the ground. The head is round compared with other breeds, with small prick ears and a short snout. Most examples in the UK are black or slate-grey (see below and colour section for illustration).

OTHER BREEDS

IRON AGE

Not strictly a breed but you may see some advertised
from time to time. They were developed by rare breeds
conservationist Joe Henson in the 1970s in response to a
request from the BBC for the type of pigs that would have
been kept during the Iron Age. He crossed Tamworth pigs
with a wild boar borrowed from London Zoo. They are
not a breed as such and there is no pedigree recording. The
Tamworth Two that caused headlines around the world in the
1990s when they escaped from an abattoir at Malmesbury
were, in fact, Iron Age pigs, not Tamworths, which probably
accounted for the fact that they eluded capture for so long.

DESCRIPTION: The Iron Age usually show common traits with
the wild boar, having stripy offspring and an unpredictable
temperament which, I would say, makes them unsuitable for
novice pig keepers (see colour section for illustration).

WILD BOAR

There are a few wild boar farms in the UK but they are not suited to a smallholder-type of operation. To keep them, you must have a Dangerous Animals Licence, which requires substantial fencing way beyond anything so far described here. Wild boar are difficult to handle and potentially dangerous and have no place in your plans.

DESCRIPTION: The Wild Boar varies in colour from brown through to almost black. It has a thick, wiry coat and small, prick ears. Unlike domestic pigs, its tail doesn't curl. The shape of a wild boar is distinctly different from the domestic varieties. It is broad in the shoulder and narrow at the hip and has a long snout with which it ploughs the ground in search of sustenance (although it will eat food and carrion found on the surface as well). Man, in developing meat producers, has emphasised the parts of the pig where the expensive cuts of meat are derived. Thus domestic pigs have much developed hams and are longer in the body, allowing for more loin chops. The shoulders are a cheap cut and thus they have been refined on the domestic pig but are there on the Wild Boar to provide strength and leverage for digging and for using his fearsome tusks for defence (see colour section for illustration).

SELLING MEAT

*This is a subject that could readily fill a book in
its own right. Here is a brief outline that will give
you some idea of the processes and regulations involved,
to help you decide how to sell the meat you've produced.*

The more involved you get in preparing and selling meat,
the more money you can make; but the health and safety
requirements in food handling increase in proportion. Food
safety is of prime importance – there are numerous regulations
and many officials enforcing them. If you start retailing your
own meat, you will be subject to all the same requirements as
the major retailers. Unlike them though, a fine of £10,000 for
a breach of the rules will have a bit more impact on you than
on a supermarket chain. You need to work carefully to ensure
that you don't break the rules and that you don't overstretch
your resources.

THE SIMPLEST, SAFEST WAY

The simplest, safest way to sell meat is to sell a complete
carcase to a butcher, or possibly a restaurant, so that your
involvement in handling the carcase is zero. You take the live
animal to the abattoir with instructions to deliver the carcase
to your customer (or for them to collect it) and, apart from
writing the invoice and cleaning your trailer, that's it. The
food handling laws do not apply to you. You should be able
to command a price that is better – by up to 40% more – than
the commercial prices quoted each week in the major farming
papers. But third parties can be slow to pay so be prepared to
nag – after all, you've had all the expense to date.

If you would like to prepare a jointed half carcase for family and friends, most abattoirs will offer to joint and pack the carcase for you but, to be blunt, many of them are a little 'industrial' in their approach and you may be disappointed that the prime pork you have so carefully produced ends up looking like a dog's dinner. I personally recommend that you get the abattoir to do what they do best, then make arrangements with a good old-fashioned butcher to do the cutting and packing for you.

If this is your chosen path, you can still avoid 'handling' the meat by getting your friends and family to collect direct from the butcher. You will have to pay both the killing charge and the butcher's invoice. You must also brief the butcher. He will need to know if the loin is to be cut as joints or broken down into chops. Should the legs be joints only or a mixture of joints and leg steaks? If joints, on or off the bone? Should he make sausages from some or all of the shoulder or belly? Does he include the trotters and offal in the half carcase pack? If you don't tell him, you may be disappointed that he couldn't read your mind. Ask your customers what they want and pass the information on to the butcher. A pensioner couple will not generally come back a second time if you gave them mostly 2.25kg (5lb) joints. Similarly a family of six won't want tiddly joints that won't make a meal.

For an animal to be butchered for onward sale to another party, it should strictly go to a licensed cutting plant where a white-coated vet can watch over proceedings. In reality, such plants are few and far between. You should check with your local authority whether they are happy for it to be done by the friendly neighbourhood butcher instead.

I recommend a pig slap marker for use when sending pigs to the abattoir. When slapped on a pig's shoulder, the device marks the pig with identification letters and numbers using sharp needle points, which it means you are more likely to get back the carcase of the pig you sent in. Plastic or metal ear tags stamped or printed with your herd mark are also useful but I still recommend the belt-and-braces method of slap marking in case for any reason the head is removed from the carcase. If you do use only tags for pigs going to the abattoir, plastic ones must be heat and flameproof so that they are legible after scalding.

HANDLING MEAT

If you do have to 'handle' the meat – perhaps because your customer can't collect and you have to deliver the packed half carcase – what's involved? I'll give you some idea but it isn't comprehensive and you will need to talk to both your local Environmental Health Officer (EHO) about food safety and your Trading Standards Officer (TSO) about labelling and more complete advice.

To handle food at any level, you should have a Basic Food Hygiene Certificate, which you gain by attending a short course and sitting a written test at the end of it. Your local council should be able to give you details of when and where these take place. This certificate is a requirement for every level of handling food so really is a must.

Next, when transporting meat, it should be done in temperature-controlled conditions and in complete cleanliness. I'm not expecting you to go out and buy a chiller van at this early stage, so you will need to do other things to show 'due diligence' – a phrase that will become familiar to you as you turn from pig farmer to retailer. Part of your briefing to your butcher will include how the meat is packaged and labelled. If it is vac-packed – not always the most attractive way to sell fresh meat, especially sausages – then there should be few difficulties in keeping things clean. If it is wrapped in freezer bags or similar, make sure they can't tear and allow dirt to contaminate the meat.

If the journey is short and the packed meat comes straight out of the butcher's chiller, then you should be able to deliver it before it starts to warm up. If the journey is longer, if you might experience delays, or it's the hottest day since records began, then you need to think about how to keep the temperature of the meat – all of it – below 8°C (46°F). A good way is to pack bags of ice between individual items. If your butcher can't provide these, many off-licences or supermarkets can. To show due diligence, measure and record the temperature at both ends of the journey and keep your records in a file.

A couple of other 'no-nos' to think about. Raw and cooked meat must be fully separated from each other. Make sure the inside of the vehicle is clean and hygienic, not where the dog usually lies or where you carried six bags of manure last week. Make sure that containers of petrol or the like are nowhere near – packs of meat smelling of the local filling station are not appetising.

I've not yet mentioned how hard you will have to work to shift this meat in terms of finding customers. If you bought two piglets and they're now porkers, obviously that's four half carcases to shift all at once. But if you're into breeding then there may well be 10 or 12 of the little blighters all coming ready at the same time. That's 20-plus customers to find, so think carefully about how you're going to market your pork. The internet's a useful resource although there's a whole heap of other producers already there and, if you're in Cornwall, do you really want to attract new customers from the Outer Hebrides? If you, your spouse or children work in a large office or factory, that can help; the personal touch fired by your own enthusiasm is a great selling tool. Similarly, your local pub or church, social or sports club can all be good places to sell your produce – although you'd need to think carefully before taking a couple of half pigs into church with you next Sunday and take care that your pub landlord doesn't ban you for undermining his food sales.

FARMERS' MARKETS

Sooner or later you'll think about doing something more proactive, like selling at a farmers' market. Now you're selling to strangers. Everything I've said about health and hygiene applies here, but even more so because you have a public image and the opportunity to poison lots more people – at least that's how the authorities see it. Firstly, don't think you can just turn up and join in. Most farmers' markets are well subscribed with purveyors of meat and there are waiting lists as a consequence.

Once you've waited your turn and got your pitch, what else do you need to consider? Well, let's think about due diligence again. The chances are that you and your meat are going to be standing there for quite a few hours. If that's not the case, either you didn't bring enough or you're selling too cheaply – your fellow marketers will undoubtedly advise you in quite strong terms if this is the case.

You need to think carefully about how to keep the temperature below 8°C (46°F). I've seen people store meat in polystyrene containers with no ice packs and hope for the best. There's no way I would ever buy from them; I fear that one day one of them is going to create such a problem that it will be a disaster for this type of retailing. So at least go armed with lots and lots of ice packs. Better still, buy yourself a chilled display cabinet. Secondhand ones are not overly expensive and you can quickly demonstrate to the Environmental Health Officer (EHO) and the public that you are doing the job right. They are, though, heavy and you will need to think about the logistics of transportation and finding an electricity supply.

Raw and cooked meat together is a big no-no so if you're cooking sausages to give out as samples, go to your EHO and ask what you need to do.

Farmers' markets are a lot of hard work. Standing around for hours on concrete while the local populace come along to grimace at your product and your prices is not a lot of fun. It is highly unlikely that you will sell everything and you will probably end up with a freezer full of odds and ends that your family don't particularly want either.

You may have ambitions to do your butcher out of a job and do the work yourself. You may think your kitchen is hygienic but it's your EHO's opinion that counts, so call him or her in to give you an inspection and be prepared to spend money (maybe lots of it), to bring your premises up to scratch.

Perhaps you'd like to open a farm shop and do the complete job in house. Again, my advice is to consult the professionals. Whatever you think it's going to cost, it will almost certainly be more, much more, so compile your business plan carefully and honestly. Where are your customers going to come from? Who's going to do the butchering and who's going to run the shop? Holiday and sickness cover? What else will you sell and where will you source it? Waste disposal? Access? Deliveries? Opening hours? Planning permission? Hazard Analysis and Critical Control Points (HACCPS)? All these and hundreds of other things need to be taken into account.

HOW MUCH TO CHARGE

We've looked briefly at most of the ways of retailing fresh meat but we haven't yet looked at pricing. Throughout this little book, I have deliberately not discussed prices because it is one aspect that can change very quickly.

But when it comes to the meat, I do believe you need guidance to do the job properly. There are many ways of arriving at a selling price. There's what's known as 'cost plus' where you write down (honestly) all your costs and then add on a percentage. Don't forget to include your labour; even if you reckon you're only worth the minimum wage – it will soon rack up.

Then there's benchmarking the competition. Going round the supermarket or farmers' market noting down the price of every cut and selling yours at the same price, slightly lower or slightly higher depending on your viewpoint. That's ok except you've not taken any account of your costs – which are likely to be very much higher per pound of pork than the commercial farmer selling squillions of pigs a year to a supermarket (and who is almost certainly losing money on every one he sells that way).

I suggest that you treat your produce with the pride that it deserves. After all, you have correctly given your pigs every advantage and the highest standards of husbandry available. If you're selling one of the rare breeds and you have mastered the husbandry so that the carcase is beautifully finished and neither too fat nor too lean, then your customers will enjoy a treat that is beyond compare. It is no accident that celebrity chefs and food writers all rave about the meat from rare breeds. The eating quality is second to none and you should be marketing a premium product. Please therefore, don't benchmark it against the cardboard sold in the mass market – not even against the supermarkets' 'best' ranges – because they don't come close to kissing the trotters of what you have produced. Price it too cheaply and your customers simply won't appreciate it. It's human nature I'm afraid, but they will only appreciate it's true worth if you sell it at a premium. So please, don't undersell your hard work and loving care – you're really only insulting your pigs if you do.

One last thing on selling meat and that's to do with labelling and advertising. In 2009 the Gloucestershire Old Spots Pig Breeders' Club (GOSPBC) won a significant and hard-fought battle against one of the supermarkets. Very briefly, the supermarket was selling bacon and sausages derived from cross-bred pigs, the sires of which were (probably) Gloucestershire Old Spots. However, the packaging and point of sale material only referred to Gloucestershire Old Spots, with the implication that the meat was from pure-bred animals. The supermarket, under pressure by now, changed the packaging and information three times, but by using words that still implied that the meat was from Gloucestershire Old Spots pigs. Eventually the GOSPBC got the body that advises Trading Standards Officers to change its interpretation and advice, closing the loopholes that allowed the supermarkets to operate this way – a significant achievement.

This standard now applies across the board and to you, too, if you're selling meat, whether direct or to a butcher. To ensure you don't fall foul of Trading Standards, remember the following:

1 To describe meat as coming from a breed, both parents must be registered pedigree.
2 If only one parent is pedigree and you want to refer to the breed, you must describe it as 'Cross-breed Large Black' or similar and the words 'Cross-breed' must be in the same style, colour, font and size as the breed name.

3 For almost all the breeds, the easiest way method of
   authentication is to birth notify every pig born with
   the British Pig Association. By doing this you can
   then download and print off a meat certificate that
   authenticates what you are selling.
4 This ruling applies to all farm animals except cattle
   so includes all breeds of pigs.

If you don't comply with these requirements, don't describe
your meat by a breed name.

Any meat that is pre-packaged must be labelled with details
of the cut provided, such as sausages or chops. Below is a
guide to the cuts of meat you will get from a pig. In addition,
the label must give guidance on storage and a best-before or
use-by date. Check with your local Trading Standards Officer
what information you need to include on the packaging.

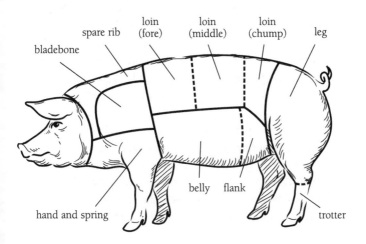

SELLING PIGS

Unlike selling pork, selling live pigs is much less fraught with problems. If you comply with everything that the authorities demand, then you shouldn't get into difficulties.

I f selling directly from your holding, the main thing to ensure is that your customers have the basics in place. They should have registered their holding and have a CPH number, which you will need to record on the Movement Licence. For your own peace of mind, make sure they have some basic understanding of what they are doing, that the vehicle they intend to transport the pigs in is suitable and that they have some proper pig food for them.

ADVERTISING

That's the legal and moral side done, but how do you find your customers in the first place? There are a number of places to advertise, many of them free. These are mainly websites, such as many of the breed clubs and country-related sites with a forum where you can place an ad direct. If you birth notify any of the breeds with the British Pig Association then you will be automatically listed and anyone searching for pigs to buy in your area will come across your details.

Away from the internet, you can advertise in the farming and smallholding magazines and in your local paper; there will almost certainly be charges for the service and delays between submitting your advertisement and the publication date. Your local feed merchants and vet's surgery may well have noticeboards where you can place a postcard with details.

You may decide to use your local livestock market, in which case you will need to contact them to find out terms and conditions such as sale days, the time you should have the pigs there, how to place a reserve and what commission and charges they will deduct. This is unlikely to be the best route for selling pedigree stock and you are likely to get less money than selling them privately; but you do away with the hassle of time wasters and it's a one-stop shop where 10 pigs should sell in one go, instead of over several weeks to a number of different buyers.

Then there are specialist pedigree sales in different parts of the country, usually during late summer and the autumn. These can be useful because they draw together a number of people with a common interest, which can lead to some spectacular prices – as well as some pretty poor ones when too few buyers are chasing too many pigs. Your breed club, the BPA or the Rare Breeds Survival Trust should be able to point you in the right direction. There should be a sale schedule including the rules spelt out in detail.

Like the meat, try not to undersell your stock. It is ridiculous that you can buy a young pedigree pig for less than 10% of the price of a pedigree puppy. I'm not suggesting that you should set your sights on the stratosphere but remember, even if it's just a hobby to you, if you sell cheaply you'll undercut everyone else trying to sell in your area and that won't make you Mr (or Ms) Popular.

COMMON PROBLEMS

*This is not a comprehensive problem-solver but
a guide to some of the more common difficulties you
may encounter when rearing pigs, from anti-social
behaviour to disappearing tattoos.*

NOTIFIABLE DISEASE OUTBREAK: I hope this never happens to you but if it does, you will receive notification – maybe not directly but via the TV news or similar – of a blanket standstill of livestock movement. This is to stop the spread of disease among farm animals and, although the regulations may seem strict and overcautious, they are in place to protect the livelihood of local farmers. However, it can seem hugely disruptive. Pigs ready for slaughter can't be moved to the abattoir and they continue eating their heads off, going 'over the top' in condition and losing value as a consequence. The pigs you thought you had sold for breeding can't be moved off your holding. Your boar is down the road on loan and you need him back urgently but he can't move. The pigs you've spent all year getting ready to show can't go and your effort has been wasted. There is nothing you can do but sit tight and listen for all new announcements on what can or cannot take place – at the same time praying that the disease in question comes nowhere near you. Incidentally, if you keep pedigree rare breeds, make sure you register your details with the British Pig Association (or Rare Breeds Survival Trust if you keep British Lops), to go on the Breeds at Risk Register. This means that your pedigree stock won't be slaughtered during an outbreak of Foot and Mouth disease as a contiguous (neighbouring) case. Your animals on your holding will only be slaughtered if they become infected. Notifiable diseases include classical or African swine fever, Foot and Mouth disease, Aujeszky's disease or swine vesicular disease – for a full list see *A Guide for New Keepers: Pigs* (see Further Reading, page 93).

EXCESSIVE ROOTING: Pigs can excavate like no other creature and if they are damaging your fields, you may need to consider ringing their snouts. The ring causes some discomfort when it is momentarily caught on roots or stones, making the pig less inclined to root. This doesn't stop the problem altogether but it does slow the process down. It's not something to try on your own, especially with adult pigs; get someone experienced to help the first time and show you what to do. It's a very noisy operation and may need to be repeated if the pig pulls the ring on a root or similar. There are several different types of nose ring for you to consider.

BOARS' TUSKS: Adult boars' tusks grow so that they emerge from the lips and can be seen pointing upwards. These are very dangerous even in the quietest boars and should be removed as soon as they are visible. The operation requires the boar to be secured by a rope with a slip knot over the upper jaw secured to a gatepost or similar; the tusks are removed using cheese wire. You should get the vet in for this job. Act promptly, preferably as soon as you see evidence of the tusks emerging.

BOARS FIGHTING: Do everything in your power, at all times, to keep two boars of sexual maturity apart. If they get together, the chances are they will fight to the death. If they do meet by accident, you will need at least three or four adults with something solid like a door to force between them. Take very great care that the humans don't get attacked by mistake.

MIXING SOWS: When you mix sows back together – usually after their piglets have been weaned – even litter sisters will 'fight' to re-establish the pecking order. It usually doesn't last long but ears may be bitten and become bloody, and it can be frightening for the novice pig keeper. To reduce the risk, introduce the stranger when the others are busy eating. By the time they've finished, the chances are the newly arrived sow may be accepted more readily. Some old books recommended covering the ears of the incomer with sump oil to cover the scent but I've never tried it.

RE-TATTOOING PIGS: If you find that the tattoos in the ears of pedigree pigs (other than Berkshire, British Saddleback, Large Black, Hampshire and other pigs that are marked with notches), become unreadable, you need to apply to the BPA or BLPS for written permission to re-tattoo. Firstly make sure the original tattoo is not there. Like small boys, pigs' ears can get fairly ingrained with dirt and you need to wash gently inside and out thoroughly (avoiding getting excessive amounts of water inside the ears). Then take a torch and, while looking inside the ear, shine the light from outside. Repeat the process the other way round and in the other ear. If there's nothing to be seen, ask permission to re-tattoo. Remember, you're not going to be able to hold the pig under your arm while you do it. He or she will need to be constrained some other way. The pressure to be applied to the tattooing pliers to mark a thick, adult ear will be much more than that needed for a pig just a few weeks' old. Lastly, the letters and numbers that filled the little pig's ear as a juvenile will hardly be seen in the adult pig's. For the best chances of success when tattooing at any age, cover the needles of the tattooing numbers with the ink paste but also apply it liberally on the ear, both inside and out, where the needles are going to penetrate, avoiding major blood vessels. This helps push the ink right through the punctures. Don't be precious about the job; be forceful in applying the pliers – you will hear a crunch as the needles go through tissue before the noise of the pig overwhelms all other senses. As you remove the pliers, you may need to ease the ear gently off the needles.

Apply more paste (which should also be an antiseptic), to both sides of the wound and rub it in. Remember the other ear too!

HEALTH: There isn't space here to list all the possible health risks so I will recommend that, as a new pig keeper, you contact the vet if you are concerned about anything. Don't let a pig suffer while you shillyshally around. As you become more experienced, you will gradually get to know which ailments require a vet and what you can treat yourself. In terms of preventative medicine, worm your pigs at eight weeks old and again every six months thereafter, making sure you note the withdrawal period (see page 10) before you send them to slaughter.

Lice are a fairly common problem especially in outdoor pigs. Use a proprietary louse powder or liquid; keep an eye out at all times for the eggs sticking to the pig's bristles around the head and neck, on the belly and inside of the legs. Ask your vet also on his or her thoughts on the need for inoculations to prevent parvovirus (which can affect fertility) and erysipelas (a potentially lethal skin infection).

USEFUL ADDRESSES

Rural Payments Agency
Tel: 0845 603 7777
*(To obtain your County Parish
  Holding (CPH) number).*

GENERAL SOCIETIES

British Pig Association
Chief Executive: Marcus Bates
Trumpington Mews
40b High Street
Trumpington
Cambridge, CB2 9LS
Tel: 01223 845100
Email: bpa@britishpigs.org
Web: www.britishpigs.org.uk

Rare Breeds Survival Trust
Executive Chairman: Tim
  Brigstocke MBE
National Agricultural Centre
Stoneleigh Park
Warwickshire, CV8 2LG
Tel: 024 7669 6551
Fax: 024 7669 6706
Email: enquiries@rbst.org.uk
Web: www.rbst.org.uk

BREED CLUBS AND SOCIETIES

Berkshire Pig Breeders' Club
Secretary: Tracey Bretherton
Eastbourne
Moss House Lane
Westby-with-Plumpton
Lancashire, PR4 3PE
Tel: 01772 685950
Email: gracebank.pigs
  @yahoo.co.uk
Web: www.berkshirepigs.org.uk

British Lop Pig Society
Secretary: Frank Miller
Farm Five
The Moss
Whixall
Shropshire, SY13 2PF
Tel: 01948 880243
Email: secretary@britishlop
  pig.org.uk
Web: www.britishloppig.
  org.uk

British Saddleback Breeders' Club
Secretary: Richard Lutwyche
Freepost (GL442)
Cirencester
Gloucestershire, GL7 5BR
Tel/fax: 01285 860229
Email: mail@saddlebacks.
   org.uk
Web: www.saddlebacks.org.uk

Gloucestershire Old Spots Pig Breeders' Club
Secretary: Richard Lutwyche
Freepost (GL442), Cirencester
Gloucestershire, GL7 5BR
Tel: 01285 860229
Email: mail@oldspots.org.uk
Web: www.oldspots.org.uk

Large Black Pig Breeders' Club
Secretary: Janice Wood
20 Alice Street, Sale
Cheshire, M33 3JF
Tel: 0161 976 4734
Email: kenworthyflock
   @fsmail.net
Web: www.largeblackpigs.
   co.uk

Middle White Pig Breeders' Club
Secretary: Miranda Squire
Benson Lodge
50 Old Slade Lane, Iver
Buckinghamshire, SL0 9DR
Tel: 01753 654166
Email: miranda@middlewhites
   .freeserve.co.uk
Web: www.middlewhite.co.uk

Oxford Sandy & Black Club
Secretary: Heather Royle
Lower Coombe Farm
Blandford Road, Coombe Bissett
Salisbury, Wiltshire, SP5 4LJ
Tel: 01722 718263
Email: OSBpigs@
   homecall.co.uk
Web: www.oxfordsandy
   pigs.co.uk

Tamworth Pig Breeders' Club
Secretary: Carolyn MacInnes
Walnut Cottage, Common Road
Wrangle, Boston
Lincolnshire, PE22 9BY
Email: secretary@tamworth
   breedersclub.co.uk
Web: www.tamworth
   breedersclub.co.uk

The Pedigree Welsh Pig Society
Secretary: Helen Tongue
Lower Nex Farm
Devauden, Chepstow
Monmouthshire, NP16 6PN
Tel: 01291 650378

Large White Breeders Club
There is no specific club for the Large White. For more information, contact the British Pig Association (see page 90 for contact details).

EQUIPMENT AND SUPPLIERS

Ascott Smallholding Supplies
Tel: 0845 130 6285
Web: www.ascott.biz
(Electric fencing, pest control, troughs and other equipment.)

Atlantic Country Superstores
Tel: 01986 894745
Web: www.atlantic online.uk.com
(Pig arks, gates and hurdles and feed hoppers.)

Fearing
Tel: 0845 600 9070
Web: www.fearing.co.uk
(Ear tags, tatooing and notching equipment.)

Schippers UK
Tel: 01733 370970
Web: www.passionfor farming.co.uk
(Heat lamps and feed and drink equipment.)

ARTIFICIAL INSEMINATION

Deerpark Pedigree Pigs
Bellaghy, Magherafelt
Northern Ireland, BT45 8LE
Tel: 028 7938 6287
Email: info@deerpark-pigs.com
Web: www.deerpark-pigs.com

FURTHER READING

Showman's Directory
Lance Publications
Park House, Park Road
Petersfield
Hants, GU32 3DL
Tel: 01730 266624
Fax: 01730 260117
Email: info@showmans-
    directory.co.uk
Web: www.showmans-
    directory.co.uk
*(Dates and contact details of all
the shows in Britain. Leading
shows where a wide selection of
pigs can be seen include the
Royal Bath & West at Shepton
Mallet, the Three Counties Show
at Malvern and the Great
Yorkshire Show at Harrogate).*

**A Guide for New
Keepers: Pigs**
*This can be downloaded free
from the DEFRA website
(www.defra.gov.uk). Search
under 'Guide for New Keepers:
Pigs' and follow the links. Print
a copy for your records, as you
should hold a copy on file at all
times and may be asked for
sight of it during an inspection
of your records.*

The Pig Site
www.thepigsite.com
*(see www.thepigsite.com/
swinenews/18969/boar-taint-an-
understanding-of-what-it-is for
more information on boar taint
and how it can affect your pigs).*

INDEX

GLOSSARY

AI: artificial insemination
BPA: British Pig Association
CPH number: County Parish Holding number
creep area: an escape area for young piglets
creep feed: special feed for piglets aged 3–6 weeks
dam: the mother pig, especially in pedigree terms
EHO: Environmental Health Officer
gilt: a young female pig
hams: the upper part of the hind legs
heritable characteristics: likely to be passed to future generations
hock: the lower part of the leg between the foot and the knee
in-pig: pregnant
loin: the mid-section of the back of the pig
maiden: term applied to a young female before being mated
NPBA: National Pig Breeders Association
pastern: the section of leg between the lower leg and the foot
RBST: Rare Breeds Survival Trust
scouring: diarrhoea
sow: a female pig that has farrowed a litter
standstill: a period during which stock may not leave your premises
to farrow: to give birth
TSO: Trading Standards Officer
underline: the two rows of teats on a female
weaner: a piglet that has been weaned